Linda Ronstadt

Linda Ronstadt

Published by Mindstir Media

1931 Woodbury Ave. #182 | Portsmouth, New Hampshire 03801 | USA

1.800.767.0531 | www.mindstirmedia.com

Printed in the United States of America

ISBN-13: 978-0-9906106-9-4

Library of Congress Control Number: 2014948654

Linda Ronstadt

ROCK'S FIRST FEMALE SUPERSTAR

written by

Mark Watson

Dedication

The author wishes to thank Tony Partridge, Mike Ronstadt,
and John Boylan - all first class gentlemen -
for their generous insights and participation.

Special thanks to original Stone Poney Bobby Kimmel for his
'Introduction' and last minute data ameliorations.

The author also wishes to thank Mrs. Patricia Watson for her
encouragement and ongoing support.

Introduction

I was really pleased when Mark Watson asked me to write the introduction to this book. I'd finally have the chance to go on record with my feelings about Linda Ronstadt and her place in popular music.

THE STONE PONEYS was a fortunate coming together of some very young musicians at the beginning of their careers. I had a body of original songs, Linda had that glorious honey-coated singing voice, and Kenny Edwards was a creative lead guitar player. It was enough to get us a recording contract with Capitol Records, and launch one of the greatest careers to ever come out of popular music.

By the time she retired 45 years later, Linda had a string of popular hits, a couple of movie themes, had sung live on Broadway, covered The Great American Song Book of the 1930s and 1940s with The Nelson Riddle Orchestra, and recorded two best-selling CDs of Mariachi songs. I can't think of anyone else from our generation who covered that kind of musical ground. And Linda did it all with uncompromising artistry!

Mark Watson tells the whole story, from the early influences of her family in Tucson, through the four decades of her career, culminating in 2014 with Linda's induction into THE ROCK & ROLL HALL OF FAME, and receiving THE NATIONAL MEDAL OF ARTS from President Obama at The White House.

Bobby Kimmel

Bobby Kimmel
Original Founding Member of THE STONE PONEYS
Tucson, Arizona / 2014

CONTENTS

★ ★ ★

1

Legend on a Stage

It is a temperate summer evening in the year 2006. More than a thousand people are gathered at Humphrey's By The Bay in San Diego, California. The mood is jubilant. Everyone has assembled to see and hear a legendary songstress perform four decades of hit songs that have made her a living icon.

The venue itself, an intimate setting positioned behind an upscale hotel on Shelter Island Drive, opened in 1982. In the quarter century since then, nearly every imaginable celebrated musician and band has graced the wooden box stage of Humphrey's.

It is approximately 7:00 and the West Coast sun is setting quickly, cooling off the day's balminess. The stage is bare except for a large black grand piano. An attractive and vivacious middle-aged Asian woman is assisting people to their respective seats. Moments later, the opening act, Wendy Waldman, appears. She is draped in all-black layered clothing with waist length dark hair. By chance, Wendy first met the show's pending headliner back when she was in high school in the early 1970s.

During the ensuing decades, despite very little commercial success, Waldman has become known within the recording industry primarily as a songwriter. Her most famous composition came to prominence in the early 1990s when her passionate ballad, 'Save The Best For Last', became

★ ★ ★

a Grammy Award-nominated triple #1 hit. As recorded by former Miss America turned singer and actress, Venessa Williams, it topped the Pop, Rhythm & Blues, and Adult Contemporary charts for weeks.

Wendy Waldman's down to Earth performance lasts about forty-five minutes. She is warm and loquacious, joking with the audience, reflecting her friendly and unpretentious demeanor. Currently in her fifties, Wendy still enjoys live performing, something the evening's headliner has always been vocal in her ardent dislike for.

Waldman finishes her set, leaving the Golden State audience primed in their anticipation of the main event. Several minutes after she departs from view, the roadies mill about, setting up musical instruments and microphones. The musicians enter the stage and take their positions. A young discovery, just out of his teens, warms up on his trumpet as the patrons sit expectantly in their seats and on the balconies of their hotel rooms. The crowd is noticeably comprised mostly of affluent, middle-aged conservatives.

Although she was never enamored with long, exhausting road trips, in 2006 Linda Ronstadt undertook what was ultimately her final concert tour.

★ ★ ★

The stage door, located at the right of the audience and leading out onto a sequestered back deck, opens and Linda Ronstadt steps inside. She is wearing black pedal pusher slacks with sandals and a matching coat with colorful embroidering. As the opening notes of 'What's New' fill the air, she saunters out to the front of the stage and the pure, affecting sound of her voice satiates those in attendance.

This is the third time that Miss Ronstadt is present for a live performance in the personal site. A few seasons prior, she had shared the stage with her close friend and fellow veteran recording star, Emmy Lou Harris. As she relays to her audience between songs, "The thing I always remember about this particular venue is watching the moon rise while I'm singing." She is truly at home in this modest yet *beau colic* Southern California atmosphere.

The first hour of music is devoted to the Jazz standards that Linda recorded with the late arranger and conductor Nelson Riddle. In fact, it was Ronstadt herself who became primarily responsible for bringing the classic compositions of the first half of the Twentieth Century to young listeners not even born when the tunes dominated the music world. The historic songs, also known as The Great American Song Book, had been in a kind of moratorium for several decades as the 1980s began. Her *What's New* album, released in 1983, went Triple Platinum (meaning it sold over 3 million copies) just in the United States. What followed was a rush of contemporary artists – from Natalie Cole to Rod Stewart – reestablishing their own careers with these extraordinary melodies.

After the first segment of the concert concludes, Ronstadt picks up the pace and launches into some of her signature hits. The songs that she belts out on this night include 'You're No Good', 'Somewhere Out There', 'Ooh Baby Baby', 'Feels Like Home', 'Poor Poor Pitiful Me' and, of course, the one she has been most identified with for nearly thirty years: 'Blue Bayou'.

By the show's conclusion, people are on their feet, many standing on their seats and others crowding the front of the stage. As the cheering grows louder, Linda exudes more intensity, moving and belting even harder to match the energy and excitement created by her electrifying presence.

★ ★ ★

After Linda and her band mates leave the stage, the fulfilled audience members casually make their way to the back of the pavilion and through the exit. Many hang around to meet and chat with the gracious Wendy Waldman who has joined the pack. The spectators have had not only a great time in the preceding hours, but they have been left with a feeling that could be described as having born witness to a historic event.

It may not have been readily apparent from the more minimalist modern day production, but the featured artist is a major superstar as well as one of the most successful recording artists of the Twentieth Century.

Linda's 2006 appearance at San Diego's intimate Humphrey's By The Bay turned out be one of her final live concert appearances.

★ ★ ★

LONG ACHIEVEMENT HISTORY

Among Linda Ronstadt's countless achievements are nineteen Gold-certified, fourteen Platinum-certified, and seven Multi Platinum-certified albums from the RIAA (Recording Industry Association of America). She is the highly acclaimed winner of twelve Grammy Awards from NARAS (the National Academy of Recording Arts and Sciences) including the 2011 Lifetime Achievement Grammy from the Latin Recording Academy. In 2014 Linda was inducted into the Rock & Roll Hall of Fame.

Linda has also amassed numerous classic hit songs on Pop, Country, Adult Contemporary, and Rock radio play lists. She was the first female singer ever to break through to a massive audience so large that she could sell out the biggest arenas and stadiums throughout the globe. This helped to earn her the well-deserved title 'First Lady of Rock'. In the narration of a special, televised 2008 tribute to her from the ALMA (American Latino Media Arts), it was affirmed that, "She is a legend. (Linda Ronstadt is) the most successful Latina recording artist in history!"

One of the most noteworthy aspects of Linda's appeal is her unwavering love of and reverence for tradition. Even in the 1970s, during her initial peak of fame, she reintroduced the work of many early renowned musicians – from Chuck Berry to the Everly Brothers to Buddy Holly – to a newer, younger listening audience. In doing this, she kept their legacy going. In a featured cover story on Linda in *Dirty Linen* magazine in 2003, T. J. McGrath acknowledged that,

> "Ronstadt opened many doors for women by being in the vanguard: the first woman to release an alt(ernative) Country album when it wasn't hip, the first true woman Rock & Roll superstar...to sell out stadiums...and the first popular female singer to go back to her roots with songs from her childhood."

Another facet of her talent is her exceptional ability with melodies and harmonies. She has an impeccable ear for them which enables her

★ ★ ★

to replicate the precise nuances of very complex song structures. She has always followed her heart in enhancing her musical instincts.

In Mark Bego's 1990 bio, *Linda Ronstadt: It's So Easy*, Linda is quoted as having stated,

> "I don't ever sing anything that isn't personal. I can only sing about my own emotions, and I always wear my emotions pretty close to the surface. I don't know how to live any other way. My image is focused because I've not on many occasions stepped too far out of character."

In the 1980s, Linda became disenchanted with Rock & Roll. She sought out new challenges to expand her abilities. Totally renovating her image at the risk of losing her established audience, she thoroughly explored and successfully transformed herself into an Opera chanteuse, a bona fide Big Band Jazz artist, and a Mariachi diva. In each of these guises, she took on the persona and aesthetic at the nucleus of the culture.

In the new millennium, Linda looked back on her initial conversion away from the Rock world and reminisced to McGrath,

> "I had been playing stadiums in front of 50,000 people, and now I was onstage singing to a smaller, more intimate audience. The Rock shows were a social and cultural happening, almost like the 'big concert event of the year' in some of the smaller cities and towns I played in. Now I was in front of a very different audience, a more sophisticated audience, and I had to work a little harder with my singing to bring them in."

That leads us to the spirit of what Linda Ronstadt is truly about. She is well known for her often exceedingly liberal views on politics, sex, and people in general. Throughout her career, she has many times courted great controversy with her outspoken statements. However, the same actions have simultaneously garnered the entertainer a substantial throng of vocal supporters for her unbridled courage in speaking out when she has seen injustice at play.

Then there's the standpoint relating to her stance as a musician. Every song Linda chooses, every note she sings, is earnest, real, and always believable. She has the aptitude of being able to sing any style, in any range, from any genre of music, while never losing the core emotion that is her trademark. If she can't relate to and learn from the experience, it doesn't infiltrate her repertoire. In the process, she relives the history and brings new life to every career choice she makes.

★ ★ ★

★ ★ ★

2

Growing Up in Arizona

The Ronstadt family history is one of pioneering achievement. Linda's paternal grandfather, Federico Jose Maria Ronstadt, immigrated to Tucson, Arizona from Mexico's capital, Senora, in the late nineteenth century with his first wife, a Mexican citizen. Tucson was established as a territory of the United States in 1853 when the Gadsden Purchase was finalized. Once Federico made his transition, he became an accomplished blacksmith and opened the F. Ronstadt Wagon & Carriage Company.

'Fred' – as he was nicknamed – became highly regarded as a pillar of the Tucson community. He was a chairman with the Tucson Chamber of Commerce and served on the Pima County Board of Supervisors. In his youth, he was said to be a gifted singer and musician, passing down his love of music to all of his children – which would eventually total eight. In 1888, Fred formed Tucson's first orchestra. They were known as the Club Filarmonico and were quite popular.

Frederico's first wife was a Mexican citizen by the name of Sarah Lavine. Together they had four children. The couple's eldest child, a daughter who went by the name of Luisa Espinel, was an international singer and dancer in the 1930s and 1940s. Residing in Spain, Espinel met and worked with famed classical guitarist Andres Segovia. Among Luisa's many accomplishments was her role in the 1935 movie *The Devil Is A Woman*, which starred Marlene Dietrich.

★ ★ ★

With his second wife, another Mexican citizen, Fred had four more children. Their four sons were William, Alfred, Gilbert, and finally Edward. The third of Fred and Lupe's kids was Gilbert Ronstadt, who was born in Tucson on the fourteenth day of June, in the year 1911. He was, of course, the father of Linda Ronstadt.

Linda's mother, Ruth Mary Copeman, was born on June 7, 1914 in Hadley Township, Michigan – located about twenty miles east of Flint – which later became Farmers Creek, Michigan. Ruth Mary's father was Lloyd Groff Copeman, who was of German Jewish descent. He was a pioneering architect with dozens of patented inventions to his credit including the electric stove, the electric toaster, and the rubber ice cube tray. Ruth Mary's mother was Hazel Berger.

Linda's mother, Ruth Mary Copeman, was born and raised in Flint, Michigan. Ruth Mary was one of the Daughters of the American Republic. She met Gilbert Ronstadt while attending Tucson's University of Arizona.

★ ★ ★

Interviewed at length for a 1984 cover story in *Family Weekly* magazine, Linda elaborated on her childhood and family members. She recalled visits to her maternal grandparents in Michigan. Regarding memories of her eccentric grandfather, she would state,

> "He used to hide under the table and grab our toes. I was terrified of him…He was very explosive and he'd get really excited and carried away. He used to lock himself in the basement for a week at time. My grandmother would bring him his meals and he'd be down there inventing the grease gun or something like that. He was one of the pioneers in developing latex."

Linda's maternal grandfather was Flint, Michigan's Lloyd Copeman, one of the most innovative and important inventors of the Twentieth Century.

In 1932, Ruth Mary was accepted to Tucson's University of Arizona. During her time at the esteemed college she met Gilbert Ronstadt, who was a fellow student. Gilbert was so smitten with Ruth Mary that he rode his

★ ★ ★

horse up the steps of her sorority one evening and serenaded her. Following a long courtship, the couple was married circa 1937 in Flint, Michigan.

The first of the couple's four children was Gretchen, nicknamed Suzi, born in March of 1939, followed by Peter Michael, who was born two years later, in February of 1941. It was five years after that when Gilbert and Ruth Mary's third child came into the world, on the fifteenth of July, a Monday, in the year 1946. They named her Maria Linda. A fourth child, Michael Joseph, arrived in August of 1953. Tucson's prominent Ronstadt family was a feature story in *Family Circle* magazine the year baby Michael was born.

The Ronstadt family has a centuries-old tradition of pioneering achievement. When Linda was seven years old, her immediate family was a feature story in Family Circle *magazine. Shown here are Linda's older brother, Peter, her father, Gilbert, her mother, Ruth Mary, her sister, Suzi, and Linda.*

Throughout her life, the couple's younger daughter would be known as 'Linda'. The Spanish origin of the name means 'pretty'. According to website BabyNamer.com, "This girl's name is used in Dutch, English, Italian, Spanish, Czech, and Swedish."

★ ★ ★

In a 1985 interview with Ron Rosenbaum for the upscale *Esquire* magazine, Linda recalled about her childhood,

> "I grew up about twenty miles outside Tucson, and at the time there wasn't a soul in sight. We lived on a dirt road with ten acres around us. I didn't go to kindergarten, so the first grade was a hell of a shock, because I didn't know any people that weren't related to me. So I was a loner. I've been this way since I was three...I think humanity is kind of horrendous but that some individuals are really nice."

Throughout her lifetime Linda has sustained a close bond with her siblings. She has periodically included them in the mechanics of her career. Shown here on stage are Peter, Suzi, Mike, and Linda.

The land and rural environment of Linda's childhood was long ago turned into residential lodging. Still, Linda forever acknowledges how fortunate she was to come from a highly functional and encouraging family unit. Reminiscing about her recently deceased and beloved mother, she stated to *Family Weekly:*

★ ★ ★

"She was wonderful. All she hoped for, I think, was that one of her children would be a scholar, and we're not scholars. Mom was always interested in everything but herself. She was never vain although she was very attractive…She liked to learn about bugs. She wanted to be a forest ranger. It makes me kind of sad. I saw a (documentary) on television, a profile of some girl forest ranger who lives up in the Yukon somewhere. I thought how my mother would have liked doing that but instead she got us. My mother never had a chance once she saw (my dad). He roped her, she was snagged and she didn't get to be a forest ranger because she was wrangling us."

Throughout her life – and continuing to the present day – the closeness of her family has provided sustenance and stability for her. She has recurrently involved them in the mechanics of her career. With three generations of Ronstadts actively involved in music, she was exposed to an amazingly broad spectrum of classic musical styles from earliest childhood. As recounted in a 1978 Linda cover story in *Country Music People*,

"Gilbert Ronstadt insisted that his children listen to more styles of music than simply whatever the current popular music happened to be…Although Linda, like most normal children, resented it at the time, she is extremely grateful now."

NUNS, PRIESTS, AND REBELLION

Although Linda was bright and articulate from the time she was a little girl, school never held her attention. The rigors of being a student in a very strict Catholic institution, in the ultra-conservative 1950s, were very difficult for her. The young girl railed against the stern authority of the nuns and priests. Boys and music proved to be continual distractions for her. She developed the reputation of being wild and rebellious. That status would stay with her throughout her school years and even through much of her adult life as well.

Following the end of World War Two, encompassing the nation's baby boom, Tucson's population was growing significantly in the Fifties. Hence, the need for additional schools to be built in the community was paramount.

Two new high schools were erected in Tucson mid-decade. Catalina High School, located on East Pima Street, opened in 1957 after three years under construction. Peter Ronstadt would be a graduate of the institution in 1959. Upon its opening, Principal Rollin Gridley told the *Arizona Daily Star* newspaper, "We are confident that Catalina is a wonderful school...the building, the student body, the faculty, and the entire personnel."

In 1957, Tucson Arizona opened Catalina High School. Linda's brother, Peter, was a charter pupil at the public learning institution. Both Linda, and her brother, Mike, followed in his footsteps, attending Catalina High. The school still stands in its original location on East Pima Avenue.

Linda Ronstadt attended St. Peter & Paul, a Catholic Parochial school from her first through eighth grades, with the exception of one year when she transferred to St. Joseph's Academy, the Catholic school where her sister, Suzi, had matriculated. She was relieved to enroll in the public Catalina High in the autumn of 1960. Attending public school relinquished her from the more stringent academic confines she had previously endured. Today Catalina High stands in the original location where Linda attended half a century ago.

★ ★ ★

In 1975, on the heels of her initial burst of big fame, Linda was still haunted by her memories of early education. She told writer Robert Windeler in an interview for *People* magazine:

"Catholic school was such an unpleasant experience for me. Those nuns still make me uptight. I never learned anything in school. Fortunately my father taught me to read at home but I still can't add. I had to jump into what I wanted to do right away. I've never had a job other than singing. If I couldn't sing for a living, I'd be stuck."

Interviewed a year later by Noel Coppage for *Stereo Review* magazine, she had this to add,

"(St. Peter & Paul) was run by the most ignorant, backward, intimidating order of nuns who shouldn't have been involved with anything except a mental hospital that they should have been patients of. They screwed me up real good!"

Despite her less than idyllic experiences in school, Linda has always maintained that her childhood was loving and stable. Her family was comprised of successful, highly educated, and caring people. Reflecting for Katherine Orloff in the 1974 book, *Rock & Roll Woman*, she said:

★ ★ ★

"My father was a singer in the Depression. The times were so hard he ended up working in my grandfather's business. My grandfather owned a ranch and my father worked as a cowboy and now (in 1974) my father has taken over the hardware business in Tucson.

By the time I came along my father was a business man but I grew up in the country. He still had an appreciation for the outdoors, a real sensitivity for the desert and for wild animals. He taught me how to shoot and ride and love the outdoors. We had horses and lots of animals and he made us fond of it all."

About the time she entered Tucson's Catalina High School in 1960, Linda started performing with her sister and older brother as The Three Ronstadts. They also performed as The New Union Ramblers. This is Linda's freshman year photo.

In 1956, ten days before her tenth birthday, Linda's maternal grandfather, Lloyd Copeman, passed away at 74. The Ronstadt family made the trip up to Michigan for his funeral. Lloyd was "kind of an intense guy" as Linda described him for a 2003 concert audience at Michigan State University. Having attended the former Michigan Agricultural College, Linda claims that "he was expelled". Copeman was a charter member of the Detroit Athletic Club in downtown Detroit and personally knew Henry Ford as well as William Durant and Charles Mott who co-founded General Motors.

★ ★ ★

ASPIRING YOUNG SINGER

When Linda was fourteen, she formed a singing group with her sister and older brother. They called themselves the Three Ronstadts at one time and the New Union Ramblers at another. It seems something of an epiphany today that she had joined her first 'trio' as they played coffee houses and fraternities in and around Tucson. They even did some recording and appeared on local television.

Not long after, Suzi Ronstadt married Alex Jacome and settled permanently in Tucson, becoming a career homemaker. She and Alex had four children together. They later divorced and Suzi remarried to Murray O'Brien. She and her second spouse had two more children together. Murray passed away in 2006 at age 81.

It was at one of the Ronstadt trio's area engagements that Linda, Suzi, and Peter met another local musician named Bobby Kimmel. Though he was about five years older than Linda, Kimmel struck up an immediate rapport with the young girl. They became good friends and he encouraged her to stay involved in music. Even after he relocated to Los Angeles, he continued to phone and write to her.

Aaron Latham, a high school classmate of Linda's, stated in a 1983 *Rolling Stone* article covering Linda in South Africa,

> "(By her teens) was already a larger than life figure with an even larger voice. She didn't surprise anyone by becoming a singer. Not that anyone expected her fame to grow to the dimensions of that voice. But the voice itself was no secret."

1964 was a fateful year for the Ronstadt family. It was the year that Linda's older brother, Peter, became a Tucson Police Officer and also got married to Jacqueline Castle from Scottsdale, Arizona. They would have two children together, Philip Charles and Melinda Marie, better known as Mindy. Mindy would grow up to sing and tour with her Aunt Linda, who left for the bright lights of Hollywood at year's end.

★ ★ ★

★ ★ ★

3

California Here I Come

In September of 1964, Linda Ronstadt began her first year of college at the University of Arizona in Tucson. Her parents had long stressed to her the importance of a good education. So, at their urging, Linda agreed to give college life a try even though she had never enjoyed the structure of academics.

Meanwhile, her friend, Bobby Kimmel, continued to contact her from Los Angeles in an attempt to lure her to the Golden State to enter the music business. Three months later, in December, she decided that college was not her mission and quit the university after only one semester. In 1975, she told Margo Jefferson of *Newsweek* magazine, "I just wasn't a student. I'd come to class occasionally in my nightgown." With her family's consent – if not exactly their blessing – Linda packed up some of her belongings, loaded her automobile and headed west.

Los Angeles in the 1960s was an aspiring and inspiring place. It was filled with talented young people yearning to break into show business. Many of them – Linda included – would go on to become legends in music. Having dreamed since early childhood of become a famous singer, she was still naïve enough to believe that anyone who seriously attempted it achieved instant fame and glory. She had a lot to learn as it

★ ★ ★

would be a long haul for the upstart. In fact, a full ten years would pass before she experienced major success and became a bona fide star. In the meantime she was ready, willing and able to go for it.

THE STONE PONEYS

Not long after arriving in the City of Angels, Linda once again joined her musical compatriot Bobby Kimmel. She settled in at 122 Hart Avenue, a white clapboard bungalow built in 1906, near the corner of Barnard Way, in the Ocean Park section of Santa Monica. The house stood 500 feet from the Pacific Ocean. Kimmel had recently met another musician named Kenny Edwards who was himself from Los Angeles. The three of them decided to form a band together. They settled on the name Stone Poneys, which they took from an old Blues song, 'Stone Poney Blues'.

Despite Ronstadt's already rather impressive and extensive pedigree in music, once in California she found her transition into becoming a professional musician to be anything but easy. There would be years of struggling ahead of her. However, the illustration of her personal road to triumph would be one in many ways akin to a storybook example.

At the same time Linda was fumbling her way around the entertainment industry, there were many other would-be musical stars in and around the same region trying to find their own method of breaking into the business. Jim Morrison, Bonnie Raitt, Sonny Bono and his then-girlfriend, Cherilyn Sarkisian LaPiere – better known as Cher, as well as members of Crosby, Stills & Nash, the Eagles, and the Monkees would all essentially graduate from the same musical school as Ronstadt.

Interviewed in 1993 for the *Los Angeles Times* newspaper, Robert Hilburn asked Ronstadt how ambitious she was as a Stone Poney. She recalled,

> "I didn't think about career at that time. I was just hoping to be able to sing and not to have to get another job. I thought I was extremely successful when I was making $80 a week because our rent was only $80 a month and we split it three ways and we lived right on the beach in

Santa Monica. There seemed to be music all around us. Jackson Browne, Tim Buckley, even the Doors lived in the neighborhood."

It was about a year after Linda arrived in Los Angeles and hooked up with her band mates, Bobby and Kenny, that they would experience their first – albeit somewhat false – step toward actual achievement. They were rehearsing above a laundromat in Ocean Park. A soul food restaurant called Olivia's Café was located across the street from the laundromat. Two wanna-be record producers were having lunch in the diner when they heard the Stone Poneys with Linda's loud and powerful voice practicing some tunes. Upon locating the aspiring trio, they gave them an elaborate pitch about being discovered and turned into instant stars. It was not to be.

The 1960s were the zenith of the nightclub era. The most famous west coast club was Doug Weston's Troubadour on Santa Monica Boulevard. Every week the venue hosted 'open mic night', where unknowns could get on stage and audition. The Stone Poneys would become regular performers at the Troubadour.

It was, in fact, through playing the nightclub circuit that the band established the following that got them noticed. The Whisky a Go-Go, the Roxy, and the London Fog were a few among the many clubs that featured the Poneys. The Troubadour was, however, the premiere launching pad of aspiring recording stars. James Taylor, the Byrds, Bonnie Raitt, Van Morrison, Elton John, and Bruce Springsteen were a just a handful of Ronstadt's fellow Rock & Roll Hall of Famers whose musical careers were launched at 'the Troub'. Comedians George Carlin, Lenny Bruce, and Steve Martin were discovered there as well.

Additionally, it was at the Troubadour where she met her first manager, a former gangster, named Herb Cohen. Cohen was a decade and a half older and would serve as a valuable mentor to the fledgling young musician. Linda would also meet subsequent manager/boyfriends, John Boylan and J. D. Souther, at the historic club.

★ ★ ★

BIG TIME RECORDING CONTRACT

It was in the summer of 1966 when Linda Ronstadt, along with Bobby Kimmel and Kenny Edwards, signed her first recording contract. Being signed to Capitol Records – one of the biggest labels in existence – was in itself a remarkable feat. Nik Venet, well-known for his production work with the Beach Boys, signed on as the group's producer. In October, the threesome found themselves in one of Capitol's historic studios laying down tracks for their debut album.

Of the eleven final tracks, eight were listed as Kimmel/Edwards compositions. In 2014, Mr. Kimmel elucidated to Ronstadt biographer Mark Watson,

> "On our first album, all the songs credited to (us) were written by me. Kenny's name was on them because there was a publishing dispute at the time. If it had ever gone to court, all the royalties would have been in Kenny's name. This was all done by our management, but I wrote all the early songs!"

Also hired to play on the record were drummer Billy Mundi as well as four additional guitarists that included James E. Bond, Pete Childs, John T. Forsha, and Cyrus Faryar. The majority of songs were pleasant and serene in tone with clear blends of harmony, but they lacked the essential 'hooks' that would capture the ears of prospective listeners.

Intent on pushing Ronstadt as the focus of the band from the start, Venet was able to get her to agree to singing three lead vocals. Her voice was up front for 'Just A Little Bit Of Rain', 'Orion', and '2:10 Train'. All three were composed by outside songwriters. Another album track, 'Wild About My Lovin'', was the most upbeat and driving song recorded for this initial product. It would have made for a more noticeable first single. It was not selected though.

Simply titled *The Stone Poneys*, the album was officially released at the end of January, 1967. The disc's opening track, 'Sweet Summer Blue And Gold', was issued as the group's debut single. Both the album and single

★ ★ ★

were non-starters, however, and failed to gain any national notice. Much of the problem was owed to the fact that the material featured on the record was far removed from what popular radio was playing in 1967. With the sounds of Motown and the huge wave of British bands dominating play lists, the gentile and ultimately 'soft' sound of the Poneys was out of sync with then-contemporary tastes.

The band continued to take gigs and work the night club circuit. They were establishing a substantial following in the LA vicinity. They were also becoming acquainted with other acts that were on the scene. But the Stone Poneys were aiming for national stardom and, therefore, the band was perpetually unhappy with their status and lack of momentum at this point. There was even a break-up between the group's first and second albums.

During a meeting with the band in the famed Capitol building at Hollywood and Vine Streets, Nik Venet discussed various strategies for the much needed breakout of the Stone Poneys. Kenny Edwards would recall, many years later, that the record producer told them, "We can make another record. We can make this happen. If we're going to do anything with this, we've got to make something that sounds commercial and get on the radio."

With that as a motivational incentive, the band returned to the studio that spring and began recording the tracks that would become the second – and most successful – Stone Poneys album.

This time around, half of the twelve tracks were listed as original band compositions - howbeit they were actually written by Bobby Kimmel - with the other half from outside writers. There would be less focus on harmonies this time around. The overall sound was more layered in texture. Also, Ronstadt's vocals were more prominent in the mixes.

BREAK-OUT HIT

Although it had been written and copyrighted in 1965, shortly before he joined the Monkees, Mike Nesmith's emotive 'Different Drum' was selected for inclusion on the group's sophomore effort. Venet was on board in his approval of the song and, according to Edwards, told the

Poneys, "This could be a hit song (but) we need to sort of have an arranger *arrange* it." That would prove to be an eventful suggestion.

The second Stone Poneys album was released to radio and to record stores in June. For the shots of the album's cover, the band was photographed at the beach with Linda in a high-waisted, long white cotton dress. It turned out to be an attractive and colorful presentation. The record's title was *Evergreen Volume Two* and initially garnered little attention. Despite the more obvious commercial potential of the tracks 'Different Drum' and 'I've Got To Know', Capitol Records surprisingly went with the moody 'One For One' as the lead single. Unfortunately it was another flop.

Ronstadt experienced her first taste of comercial success as a member of The Stone Poneys, a Folk-Rock band she formed with Bobby Kimmel, left, and Kenny Edwards, right, not long after moving to Los Angeles in the mid-1960s. However, her record label and management were only interested in promoting Linda. The group disbanded in 1968.

Over the summer 'Different Drum' had started to gain some attention from radio programmers, especially in California. This was due, in part, to the enormous sensation the Monkees were during 1967. Belatedly, in September, the Poneys version of 'Different Drum' saw the light of day and was released as a single or '45'. (During the 1960s and 1970s, seven-inch 45 RPM records were the biggest selling format and outsold twelve-inch vinyl albums.) It was a sleeper hit to be sure but gradually picked up steam. In November, the band finally made their debut on the national record charts.

★ ★ ★

Billboard and *Cash Box* were the dominant forces in industry publications, better known as 'trades'. They were music biz powerhouses.

Radio airplay and sales of 'Different Drum' continued to grow and spread throughout markets across the United States. Early in 1968 the song reached a sizable #13 in *Billboard*. It spent a healthy nineteen weeks on the Top 100 in *Cash Box* where it climbed to #12. (In the Detroit marketplace, it got as high as #6.)

Evergreen Volume Two entered the *Billboard* album chart several weeks after 'Different Drum' made its debut and logged a respectable fifteen weeks on the listing. The Stone Poneys were finally getting noticed. Although there were no television appearances, Capitol sent the Poneys out on the road opening for Jim Morrison's group, the Doors, on the heels of their massively successful chart-topping album and million-selling hit 'Light My Fire'. Regrettably, the reception that Kenny, Bobby, and Linda received was far less than stellar as the Doors had a more aggressive sound, appearance, and following.

Similarly, what seemed to be an auspicious breakthrough with 'Different Drum' was leveled when the next single, 'Up To My Neck In High Muddy Water', stalled at #93 in the early spring of 1968. (Their fifth and last single failed to chart at all.) The Stone Poneys continued to play the clubs, such as a week-long engagement at the Bitter End in Greenwich Village but their struggle continued. There were, in fact, numerous break-ups for the trio throughout their tenure together.

In early 1968, while the Poneys were laboring over their third – and final – album release, Kenny Edwards quit the band and moved to India. Released in April, *Stone Poneys And Friends Volume Three* failed to chart despite the recording having a more mainstream sound and increasing focus on their shy but intriguing girl singer. In fact, the front cover of the album featured only Linda in a colorful, wind-blown snap shot .

Ronstadt had long dreaded becoming a solo artist. Strikingly timid on stage, she spent her share of time experimenting with recreational narcotics. She was especially fond of cocaine. One must bear in mind that during this era drug use was not only a dominant fixture throughout most circles of the entertainment industry but also a widespread movement in California, particularly among the youth culture. Linda was merely assimilating with the crowd.

With the disbandment of the Stone Poneys in 1968, Linda found herself obligated to fulfill the seven year recording contract that was in place. Although very unsure of herself and her artistic abilities at this point in time, she begrudgingly began recording her first solo album for Capitol.

Even though the band had exemplified the sound of Folk Rock, their final record had contained elements of Country music. Linda decided to embrace her Country music influences more fully now that she was on her own. Containing a patchwork of Country and Pop/Rock fundamentals, the album *Hand Sown/ Home Grown* was unleashed in the spring of 1969. This time the most commercial track, 'The Long Way Around', was selected for release. In spite of national network appearances on *The Tonight Show with Johnny Carson, Playboy After Dark,* and a John Byner special, both the single and album were failures.

In these formative years, Linda's career was given a boost by a Country music legend named Johnny Cash. Cash was taken with the carefree and uninhibited young underling and had her on his highly rated television variety show five different times in his three years on the air. Linda, who loved wearing ultra-short skirts but never wore undergarments, caused quite a stir. According to the show's makeup artist, Penni Lane,

> "At rehearsal, June Carter Cash noticed that Linda didn't have any panties on, so she came running back to the dressing room, saying, "Somebody get down the street and buy her some bloomers. She's out there showing herself!"...When Linda was told she would have to wear underwear (for the actual taping) she was very upset!"

Mr. Cash's longtime manager, Lou Robin, was also present during Linda's appearances on *The Johnny Cash Show*. Asked if he had ever witnessed any such incidents, he recalled,

> "That was true. June wasn't too thrilled about it. That was Mrs. Johnny Cash speaking out. But Linda was a free spirit

★ ★ ★

and she sure could sing. John really enjoyed having her... She made a total of five appearances... She would always come in barefooted (as well as pantyless and braless), which was thought to be kind of unusual in those days."

The musical future of Linda Ronstadt seemed somewhat bleak as she rolled along with her singing career. Continuing along the path of merging the rudiments of Rock and Country, at the start of the Seventies she went to Nashville, Tennessee – the capitol of Country music – to record her second solo album. Though the musicians hired for the task were highly qualified, they had never played with Ronstadt. There was little symbiosis to the project and she had yet to find her true voice. Like the previous recording, it was a somewhat empirical exercise in sonic experimentation.

To further prove the point, Linda was more than willing to experiment with her image. The album was given the offbeat title of *Silk Purse*, a pun on the old adage 'You can't make a silk purse out of a sow's ear.' The cover featured her sitting in a pigsty surrounded by pigs and wearing ultra-short cut off blue jeans with a sheer light pink blouse. There was increasing attention being focused on this winsome braless, pantiless, and barefoot lorelei. A giant billboard replica of the picture was erected on Sunset Boulevard for promotion.

An outtake from the 1970 Silk Purse *photo session. Ronstadt was attempting a humorous spoof on her early image as another Moonbeam McSwine.*

★ ★ ★

In an attempt to spur record sales and ignite her career, Linda again appeared on The Johnny Cash Show in the spring of 1970 singing her unusual remake of the classic 'Will You Love Me Tomorrow?' As a perpetuation of promoting the singer in the Country music idiom, she was even booked to appear on an episode of *Hee Haw* around this time. Her single peaked at #98 in *Cash Box* and briefly made *Billboard*'s Bubbling Under The Hot 100 chart. Several weeks later, radio stations in Los Angeles began to notice a dramatic ballad featured on *Silk Purse*.

Entitled 'Long Long Time', it displayed a remarkably powerful vocal from the diffident twenty-three year old ingénue. 'Long Long Time' was aching with emotional intensity but Capitol execs were reluctant to put it out on a single. After much cajoling from the artist, they eventually relented. Released in June, it finally made the charts in August. While the fervent tune was slow in its ascent, it eventually climbed as high as #25 on the Pop chart and even cracked the Top 20 at Easy Listening radio. (Ironically, it received no attention from Country radio where it seemed most suited to.)

Silk Purse had been in the record stores since March, but it didn't make the album chart until October – seven months after release. Even with the success of 'Long Long Time', it climbed no higher than #103. Early the following year, Linda Ronstadt found herself seated in the second row at the first televised Grammy Awards celebration. She was nominated alongside Diana Ross, Anne Murray, Dionne Warwick, and Bobbie Gentry for the Best Contemporary Vocal Performance Female trophy in her first nomination. It was proof positive that the music world was indeed taking notice of her talent. In time she would become one of the most honored artists in Grammy history.

A ROCKIN' NEW BAND

It was also during early 1971 that Linda met and assembled several aspiring musicians at the Troubadour who would be instrumental in her career as well as her artistic development. Glenn Frey had moved to California from Royal Oak, Michigan, where he was born and raised.

★ ★ ★

Don Henley had dropped out of the University of Texas and headed to the West Coast, while Randy Meisner had come down from Nebraska. Bernie Leadon, who had been playing behind Linda for some time, completed the core of her new back-up band. In 1972 they would split from their girl boss and become the legendary Eagles. In the meantime, they conjoined at Capitol studios in March to begin sessions for the eponymous album *Linda Ronstadt*.

Linda's handlers capitalized on her sexuality from the beginning, playing up her innocent expression. It was a plausible marketing angle promoting her as the embodiment of a carefree creature. She never wore a bra and only occasionally wore panties. Fellow musicians reported that she sometimes recorded topless in the studio.

As the wild and crazy Seventies continued, Ronstadt was making slow headway in the industry. In what was still a tight industry, where performers basically all knew one another, essentially every other singer in the business knew Linda's name. But super-stardom was still several years away.

During this time she made her debut – with the future Eagles behind her – at North Hollywood's famed Palomino Club on Lankershim Boulevard. Although the club seated a modest 400 patrons, it was known as Country music's most important west coast venue where everyone from Johnny Cash to Merle Haggard to Buck Owens played regularly. Noted

★ ★ ★

Journalist Robert Hilburn reviewed Linda's appearance at the nightclub for the *Los Angeles Times* that December, stating:

> "The Palomino Club no doubt has seen few evenings as spirited as the one in which Linda Ronstadt made her debut. In direct contrast to the conservative stereotype of the girl Country singer, Miss Ronstadt raced on stage the other night wearing a tight red sweater (with) sequined blue jean hot pants, and asked the waitress to bring a supply of tequila for her and the band."

Hilburn's review was glowing. Interestingly, in the face of detailing her lineage in the field of Country music, she was classified as a Rock artist in his article. Adding to the attention placed on her physical appeal, he elaborated:

> "The regular Palomino customers seemed simply overwhelmed as she began…But it wasn't so much the music that caught the audience's attention. It was she. Tammy Wynette may sing 'Stand By Your Man' with unbeatable intensity but she never looked like Miss Ronstadt."

Despite being very unsure of herself onstage in the early years of her career, Linda's stage presence gradually became more poised as time evolved.

★ ★ ★

The *Linda Ronstadt* project was her third outing as a solo act. Held up from the public until January of 1972, it included several high energy tracks recorded live at the Troubadour, including a super charged version of 'Rescue Me'. With a high caliber assortment of material and musicianship, the album was touted as Ronstadt's imminent major breakout. But to the chagrin of everyone involved – especially the artist – it was another commercial failure. The record peaked at #163 on *Billboard*'s album chart. Its sole single release, 'Rock Me On The Water', written by up and coming songwriter Jackson Browne, stalled at #85 on the Hot 100. Strongly vocal to the press and fellow performers over the failure of the venture, she made the decision to sever her relationship with Capitol Records.

Over the years, Ronstadt has stated in numerous interviews that it was not her intention to be a superstar and that she merely wanted to make quality music. In reality, though, that sentiment acts as a form of pseudo modesty. Despite a professed lack of confidence in her abilities during her years at Capitol, she had the drive and the talent and therefore possessed the expectation of being catapulted into the major leagues. She was growing restless waiting for major success.

Fortunately with her pending move to a new record label and her discovery of a new manager and producer, it wouldn't be much longer until Linda Ronstadt ruled the record charts, the airwaves, and the world.

★ ★ ★

★ ★ ★

4

#1 Female Singer

Linda Ronstadt's musical career had been erratic, but as she moved into the middle of the 1970s, the recompenses of her vocation were heating up. Her 1973 release, *Don't Cry Now*, was her most successful recording to date. By the time her next album came out in late 1974, *Don't Cry Now* had sold upwards of 300,000 copies. She had also gained additional exposure through major network television appearances on shows like *The Midnight Special* and as the opening act for Neil Young's highly successful *Harvest* tour.

Regardless, her life was far from stable and happy. Linda's two record labels, Capitol and Asylum, would now fight over her for more than a year. She was in debt to two managers and experiencing emotional havoc over her personal life as well. She was living in a West Hollywood apartment that rented for $150 per month and had to haul her own laundry to the Fluff & Fold Laundromat on Cahuenga Boulevard in North Hollywood as she didn't own a washer or dryer. The day was saved when Peter Asher, an effectual artist manager and record producer – as well a former Pop star – stepped in to finish the last several tracks on *Don't Cry Now*. Shortly thereafter, Asher agreed to sign on permanently as Linda's new producer as well as her personal manager.

What made the dynamics between Linda and Peter different from her past alliances was that he was the very first manager and/or producer that

★ ★ ★

she was not involved with sexually. She confessed to Katherine Orloff in 1974, "I have a manager now I'm *not* having a relationship with." Since first moving to California, a decade earlier, she had never employed representation with anybody that she wasn't intimately involved with. That had caused a lot of complications for her.

As Linda's career evolved, she worked diligently at developing her voice and expanding her level of musicianship. She increased her skills on the guitar, piano, and violin.

In June of 1974, Asher and Ronstadt began recording sessions for her next album. She had inked with – initially as a contingent act – David Geffen's hot new label, Asylum. That was the record label that issued *Don't Cry Now*. But executives at Capitol Records were very unhappy with her. They were planning to pursue legal action to recoup their financial losses if the situation wasn't rectified in short order. After numerous meetings with Capitol representatives, it was finally agreed upon that the label would be able to choose any one of Linda's next three albums for their own. (Naturally, they would choose the irresistible *Heart Like A Wheel*.)

It quickly became obvious that everything was not only on track with the new sessions but that there was a kind of magic present in them. A brilliant, red-haired musician in his early twenties named Andrew Gold

★ ★ ★

had joined the band for this recording and his skill was phenomenal. In addition to Andrew, former Stone Poney Kenny Edwards returned to the fold. He would be a core member of her recording and touring band, lasting throughout Ronstadt's Rock & Roll reign. In 2011, following Gold's early death, she recalled meeting him for the first time, "He came up to talk…He was so bubbly and so smart and we (the Stone Poneys) were so impressed with what a good musician he was."

Among the songs that Linda had been performing in her live sets was a little known Soul music gem called 'You're No Good'. It had been a Top Ten R&B hit for black songstess Betty Everett a decade earlier but was not known to the general listening public. Ronstadt's searing version of 'You're No Good' would quickly climb to the #1 spot on both the *Billboard* and *Cash Box* music charts. It put her over the top, lighting off one of the biggest hit making streaks ever accomplished in popular music.

FIVE STAR CLASSIC ALBUM

Linda's new album was titled *Heart Like A Wheel*. It included elements of Rock, Blues, Country, Folk, and Pop. For the rest of her career the album would be considered her lifetime masterpiece. Linda's voice had matured into a ripe and seductive instrument with tremendous control. Moreover, the timing was finally right for her to experience a major breakout.

Released in the final weeks of 1974, *Heart Like A Wheel* exploded at the start of 1975. Just a few weeks into the new year, Linda Ronstadt was #1 in both *Cash Box* and *Billboard* – giving her the most popular and biggest selling album and single in the United States. Decades later, in the year 2006, writer Chris Smith would publish his book *100 Albums That Changed Popular Music*. One of those influential hundred discs was the five-star classic *Heart Like A Wheel*. In 2014, the Library of Congress entered *Heart Like A Wheel* into the National Recording Registry.

The album and its sizzling hits blasted Ronstadt into the top tier of recording artists along with acts like Led Zeppelin, Elton John, and the Eagles. The follow-up single to 'You're No Good' was a rollicking remake of the Everly Brothers' 'When Will I Be Loved?' It hit #1 in both Pop and Country and became one of her most treasured hits. She had never much enjoyed doing television but Linda made numerous small screen appearances during 1975 to support her new eminence as a recording star.

COPING WITH STARDOM

Along with her newfound celebrity status came a lot of unwelcomed attention. She was suddenly all over the pages of magazines and newspapers which were then the main outlets for entertainment information. She could no longer go about every day activities such as going out to eat, shopping, and getting groceries or gasoline without being recognized and hounded by fans.

Linda confessed to being miserable in copious interviews during this time frame. As she arrived at the summit of the record charts, becoming a million-selling *artiste* in the process, it was evident that she felt anything other than a strong sense of pride in her accomplishments. *Rolling Stone* magazine did their first of an eventual six cover stories on her as she experienced her initial takeover. She candidly offered to writer Ben Fong-Torres:

> "I don't know, I may be just an unhappy person forever. I'm very dissatisfied with everything. I'm hard to please and very restless, so it's always a battle between that and my real deep desire to have a home and roots, which is a kind of contentment which is beyond description when you find it. I've only had glimpses of it."

Discussing the topic of love and romance in the same interview, she also relayed this sentiment to the *Rolling Stone* writer:

> "People commit suicide without it. I was reading a study that showed people did it because they couldn't make an intimate connection with another human being. You need that – or else it's religion or drugs. I could never handle

religion. And drugs – there's no way out of that…I had to have my nose cauterized twice. I think they shot sodium nitrate up there."

From a business perspective, however, the conquest of *Heart Like A Wheel* paid off all monies owed to her ex-managers and former recording label thereby fulfilling the obligations of her Capitol recording contract once and for all. In addition, her live concert audience which had steadily grown larger over the past couple of years, increased dramatically. 1975 found Linda Ronstadt selling out the top venues in the United States including Michigan's Pine Knob which was then the biggest outdoor pavilion in the country. Coincidentally, 'the Knob', as it was called, was located on Sashabaw Road, not far from where her maternal grandparents had lived and where her mother had grown up.

Linda found the sudden influx of concentrated attention on her hard to accept. She was self-conscious and overwhelmed by the public interest in her. That year she sought out a psychiatrist (She had also admitted to seeing one in her first *Rolling Stone* interview.) in Los Angeles to assist her in dealing with this scrutiny. It helped her deal with her internal issues and to move forward with her now lofty career.

One thing that seemed to set Miss Ronstadt apart from other girls in the music business was her naturalness. Unlike other female performers, past and future, there had been no decided *image* created for her. Linda was just naturally Linda. She was always frank and completely free of artifice. Dick Clark later described her as exuding "coquettish sex kitten charm". The media and music fans found her down-to-earth veracity to be astoundingly refreshing. She had a shy yet flirtatious demeanor that people loved. Her expression was often sad, almost vulnerable. She appeared sweet and innocent.

While seeking professional help, Linda was also busy recording and preparing another album. She was now an exclusive agent of Asylum Records and the company was filled with pride over its latest luminary. Linda had been performing a Motown classic called 'Love Is Like A Heat Wave', which was made famous by Detroit's group Martha & The

Vandellas, in her live shows for some time. Though she never felt it was one of her stronger vocal exercises, David Geffen loved the gritty way she sang it and the reaction to it from her live audiences. He visited Linda in the studio and told her she needed to record the tune as it was a surefire hit. She had serious doubts but Geffen would be accurate in his prediction.

Ronstadt's 1975 album release was *Prisoner In Disguise*. The title track was an intensely somber composition by her former boyfriend, J. D. Souther. Another classic song that she covered this time was 'I Will Always Love You' written by her idol and new friend, Dolly Parton. Dolly was already one of Country music's brightest stars but would go on to staggering international distinction, eventually eclipsing even Linda's fame.

Irresolute about which song to choose for *Prisoner*'s first single, she decided on 'Love Is A Rose' from her old buddy, Neil Young. It was released to radio and record stores in mid-August and was climbing both Pop and Country charts when another cut with the shortened title 'Heat Wave' began receiving airplay. Not wanting to lose 'Love Is A Rose' in the shuffle, Asylum pulled it off the market and issued 'Heat Wave' – with 'Love Is A Rose' as the flip side – in early September. The decision proved fruitful as 'Heat Wave' quickly climbed into the Top Five on the Pop side (it was also hugely popular on burgeoning AOR radio) while 'Love Is A Rose' hit the Top Five at Country radio.

Prisoner In Disguise never attained the same level of popularity that *Heart Like A Wheel* did, but it was another success. It was certified Gold within days of entering *Billboard*'s album chart and rapidly became Ronstadt's second consecutive million-selling album. In fact, Linda would close out 1975 as the year's #1 female artist with three Gold albums (*Don't Cry Now* had passed 500,000 in sales over the summer), surpassing major hit makers Olivia Newton-John and Helen Reddy.

It was a fact that 1975 changed Linda's life forever. *People* magazine ran a story on her that fall and reported that "1975 will be remembered as the year when Linda Ronstadt belatedly happened." The publication also detailed the Malibu, California beach house and lavish automobiles she purchased at the time. Fame was a culture shock for her, to be sure, but

★ ★ ★

in the coming years she would adjust to the status of being a pampered celebrity. Much later in her career, she would gain the reputation of being a difficult and demanding diva.

1976 began on a high note for the now twenty-nine year old star. As the year began she was climbing the Pop, Easy Listening, and Country charts with her latest hit, another classic Motown remake, Smokey Robinson's 'Tracks Of My Tears'. The selection seemed a mismatched choice for her but she sang it with plenty of her trademark emotion and genuineness.

When the Grammy Award nominations were announced, Linda Ronstadt was back in the running for the first time in five years. This time she found herself up for trophies in not one, but several major categories. *Heart Like A Wheel* was nominated for both Best Pop Vocal Performance Female and the year's most important category, Album Of The Year, alongside Elton John, The Eagles, Janis Ian, and Paul Simon. Many critics predicted that she would walk away with both honors. However, she lost out to Janis Ian and Paul Simon respectively.

She did, however, take the prize for Best Country Vocal Performance Female for the song 'I Can't Help It (If I'm Still In Love With You)' which had reached the top of the Country chart a year earlier. She was chosen over Dolly Parton, Loretta Lynn, Emmy Lou Harris, and Jessi Colter. Linda was now officially a Grammy Award winner which added to her clout in the industry.

The following month Ronstadt began recording her third album for the Asylum label. Despite her success – or perhaps because of it – she was admittedly "very depressed" at times. The new recording, which she would call *Hasten Down The Wind*, was largely solemn in tone with many songs about unrequited love. Three of the tracks – 'Lose Again', 'If He's Ever Near', and 'Someone To Lay Down Beside Me' – were written by former Bryndle band member and Linda's new Malibu Colony neighbor, Karla Bonoff. The title cut, 'Hasten Down The Wind', was written by another up and coming talent, Warren Zevon.

The *Hasten Down The Wind* scheme was notable for another reason as well. Although she had felt more confident interpreting the work of

★ ★ ★

other songwriters, Linda herself had the inherent talent of composing. As she stated in *People* in 1975, "I'd hate to add to the ever increasing pile of bad songs." But in 1976, she herself composed two tracks, 'Try Me Again' and the Spanish-language 'Lo Siento Mi Vida' for her latest recording. Asked about her official songwriting debut that year, she told *People*, "There's nothing wrong with throwing something against the wall to see if it sticks."

An outtake from Linda's sexy Rolling Stone *magazine photo shoot in 1976. She graced the cover of* Rolling Stone *a total of six different times between 1975 and 1980.*

ROCK'S FEMALE SEX SYMBOL

As her fame continued to spread, Linda was increasingly acknowledged as Rock & Roll's female sex symbol. In the 1990s, introspective writer Karen Schoemer looked back and described Miss Ronstadt as "the undisputed Queen of Rock: sexy and feisty at the same time...a poster girl for free-wheeling femininity." She stood little more than five feet

★ ★ ★

tall, with big dark expressive eyes, silky long black hair, and a cute little figure. She was the ideal embodiment of the sexual revolution. In a 1976 interview with *The Boston Phoenix*, Linda revealed that:

> "I find that as I get older, my sex drive increases more and more...I've always had this virginal concept of sex, that you should only go to bed with someone you were madly in love with...I've decided that the best reason to go to bed with somebody (is) pure love, which includes friendship...after that (is) pure *lust*. The third reason would be curiosity...I've decided that all of those reasons are valid!"

Linda Ronstadt was the music world's premier female sex symbol of the 1970s during the height of the sexual revolution. She was a free spirit who was completely relaxed with her sexuality. Famed celebrity photographer, Annie Liebowitz, worked with Linda on many occasions.

As usual, Linda spent much of her calendar year touring, traveling throughout the United States. She also undertook her first major trek through Europe. As a result, she established a moderate following on the continent. Accompanied by the premier single, a remake of Buddy Holly's 'That'll Be The Day', the *Hasten Down The Wind* album was unleashed to her expectant public in August. The response was extremely enthusiastic. Within days of release, it was certified Gold. By late October it was certified Platinum, making it her fastest selling record yet. She was the

★ ★ ★

first female artist in history to score three consecutive million-selling albums. No doubt aided by the revealing and suggestive album cover photos, *Hasten* shot to #1 on *Billboard*'s Country albums chart and #3 on the Pop albums chart.

As proof of her growing standing among musicians, late that year Ronstadt earned her second *Rolling Stone* magazine cover. There was less confessional declaration in the text this time, but the racy photos of her – in evocative poses wearing a red teddy – stirred some uproar. Tabloids went wild with salacious cover stories about her. *Modern People* later published an issue with one of the carnal images on its cover and the caption: "Linda Ronstadt's Private Sex Life-The Untold Story That'll Knock Your Socks Off!" Inside, the heading read: "Linda Ronstadt: Let's Pray She Doesn't Become A Hooker!..."

In December, just in time for the Christmas holiday season, Asylum released Linda's first *Greatest Hits* package. It chronicled her first ten years of hits from 'Different Drum' to 'That'll Be The Day'. This album would become the most popular disc of her entire career, selling in massive quantities for decades to come. In 2001, it was certified seven times Platinum for sales over seven million US copies.

PINNACLE OF SUCCESS

Ronstadt's success continued to snowball in the next year. It was now 1977. In January, Jimmy Carter was sworn in as the thirty-ninth American president. He publicly acknowledged Linda Ronstadt as one of his personal favorites and loved the way she sang 'When Will I Be Loved?' By invitation, she performed at President Carter's televised inaugural celebration singing 'When Will I Be Loved?' and Patsy Cline's perennial 'Crazy'. She was uneasy and stiff but it increased her recognition factor. Mr. Carter would not be the last United States President who would request her to sing for him.

Early in the year she was the featured cover story of the heralded *Time* magazine. Illustrated with numerous color photos of its subject scantily clad, the article was highly revealing. It openly discussed everything from

★ ★ ★

Linda's use of illegal narcotics to her hyperactive and adventuresome love life. About her recent White House performance, she opined, "I was so nervous. My God, I was awful!" At the 1977 Grammy Awards she was the predicted winner for the Best Pop Vocal Performance Female statuette. When she walked away with it, she left Joni Mitchell, Natalie Cole, Emmy Lou Harris, and Vickie Sue Robinson in the dust.

Following her massive breakout as a chart-topping superstar in 1975, Ronstadt starting winning Grammy Awards - which are the recording industry's highest achievement. In 1977, Ringo Starr presented her with the statuette for Best Pop Vocal Performance Female. Having won a record 11 competitive Grammys, Linda stands as one of the most recognized female recording artists in history.

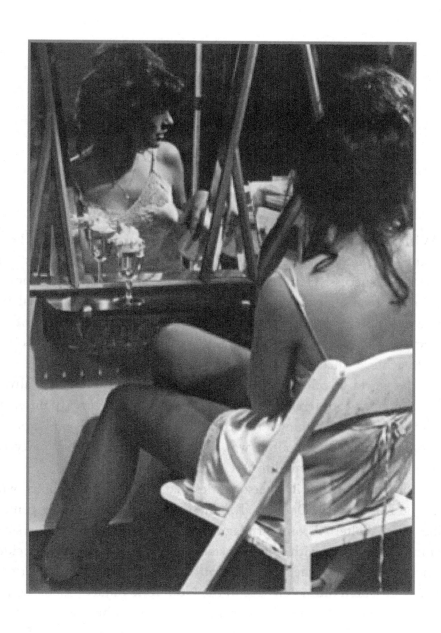

★ ★ ★

5

The Queen of Rock

With non-stop media coverage, including cover stories in *People,* *US,* and *Rolling Stone,* the year would find Linda Ronstadt at the very pinnacle of success. Her romance with Jerry Brown, the Governor of California, made her an even more high-profile and controversial figure. Even though she frequently complained about the invasion of her privacy, this was the powerful position that Linda Ronstadt had worked hard to achieve since coming to Hollywood in 1964.

In the world of celebrity, different components of fame have always had a tendency to interact. Musicians, actors, sports figures, politicians, and so on meet and comingle together. By 1977, Linda was undoubtedly a priority 'A List' superstar. She was, undeniably, the proverbial party girl who was regularly seen at elite 'A List' functions.

Among the non-musical personalities that her fame had collided with were the Los Angeles Dodgers. Tommy Lasorda took over management duties from Walter Alston that year. A number of the team members had become so enamored with Miss Ronstadt that it was unanimously decided to invite her to sing the National Anthem during the World Series – which they would ultimately lose to the New York Yankees. Looking like a shapely mouthwatering desert, in tight jeans and a blue satin Dodgers jacket, Linda belted out 'The Star Spangled Banner' in front of 56,000 live baseball fans – and many more millions of television viewers – with

★ ★ ★

vehemence and plenty of gusto.

Linda's status as a high profile superstar made her an A List luminary. In the 1970s, she earned the reputation of being quite the party girl and was a frequently seen figure at celebrity parties and functions. Ronstadt is shown here with Led Zeppelin's Robert Plant and The Rolling Stones' Ron Wood in 1977.

The album that she released that year was titled *Simple Dreams* and it was one of her biggest sellers ever. It pushed Fleetwood Mac's *Rumours* out of #1 on *Billboard*'s album chart after twenty-nine weeks at the summit. 1977 was also the year that Elvis Presley died. Due to the sales boom of Elvis records immediately following his passing, two albums – *Moody Blue* and *Elvis In Concert* – kept him locked in at #1 on the County albums chart for fifteen straight weeks. In December, *Simple Dreams* knocked Presley out of the top slot on that chart. In fact, *Simple Dreams* sold more than three and a half million copies in the United States alone in less than a year. That was far more copies than either of the two Elvis discs ever sold.

Simple Dreams produced a slew of major hits. The first of them, 'Blue Bayou', turned out to be the biggest selling single of Ronstadt's entire

★ ★ ★

career and her signature song for the rest of her life. It was certified Gold (for sales of over a million copies in America) during its chart run. It would continue to sell, going Platinum (for US sales of over two million) in 1990. 'Blue Bayou' reached the top of the Pop, Country, and Easy Listening charts, and stands as one the great classic moments in music history.

As 'Blue Bayou' was climbing the charts, the listening public couldn't get enough of Linda Ronstadt. Radio stations were flooded with requests for her songs. Music stores couldn't restock her records quickly enough. Another track from *Simple Dreams,* a Buddy Holly remake called 'It's So Easy', was instantly so popular that Asylum Records had little choice but to issue it on a 45 also. Linda became the first female singer in history to have two songs in the Top 10 at the same time. In fact, both 'Blue Bayou' and 'It's So Easy' spent the entire month of December in the Top Five.

Ronstadt was the first female singer to build an audience large enough to fill stadiums and arenas worldwide. In later years, she would deliberately downsize to smaller, more classy venues.

Although there were some lingering insecurities in Ronstadt's psyche, she had noticeably progressed as a vocalist, artist, and live performer. Her confidence level had grown considerably. Music critic John Rockwell published an in-depth depiction of her life and persona in *New Times* that fall. In the article, Linda told Rockwell:

★ ★ ★

"Lots of times I've felt I haven't gotten enough credit for the arrangements. Lots of times I feel I haven't taken enough responsibility. What I did on this album was pick the musicians, pick the tunes, pick the style of the arrangements, and then just let everybody do their job – and it worked. I think *Simple Dreams* is a great statement about California music."

In the early 1970s, Linda formed a tight friendship with fellow singers Dolly Parton and Emmy Lou Harris. The professional relationship of the 'Trio' would last for decades, through two hugely successful albums and many television appearances. In January of 1978, the ladies convened in Music City to record their first full album together. Ronstadt and Harris stayed at Dolly's Nashville home for ten days.

As anticipated, in early 1978, Linda was again nominated for Grammys in several top categories. The winner of the previous year's Best Pop Vocal Performance Female, she was nominated for it the third consecutive time. She was expected to win it again for 'Blue Bayou' but when the

★ ★ ★

envelope was opened, the name Barbra Streisand was announced. 'Blue Bayou' was also nominated for Record Of The Year but the Eagles smash 'Hotel California' took the accolade instead.

ROCK QUEEN ON THE BIG SCREEN

For the past couple of years Linda Ronstadt had been receiving offers from movie studios to star in major motion pictures. None of the scripts held her interest though. She was proposed top billing alongside Robert Redford in *The Electric Horseman* but turned it down. The role went to Jane Fonda instead. Still, in 1978, she made her big screen debut in the film *FM*. The plot centered on QSKY, a fictitious LA radio station and starred several big names including Eileen Brennan, Martin Mull, and former Detroit Lions football player turned actor, Alex Karras. The movie enjoyed a long run in theatres, and was popular enough to inspire the television series *WKRP In Cincinnati* which ran from 1978 to 1982.

Writer Mary Ellen Moore provided her review of the film in *The Linda Ronstadt Scrap Book* later that same year, stating:

> "The real star of the show is Linda Ronstadt…It's Linda at her best, giving all her fans who have had to be content with far-off glimpses of her at over-sized concert halls a real close-up look at the Rock & Roll Queen…All of the attributes connected with Linda came across in the film: her vulnerability, her sexiness, her abundant talent, her cuteness, her slightly ill at ease stage presence."

Linda's romance with Governor Jerry Brown heated up during this era as well. The couple garnered ongoing front page publicity as a result. In the spring of 1979, they traveled to Africa on what was supposed to be a private vacation. Instead, the pair was pursued relentlessly by the media. The trip made headlines all over the world with photographs of the couple featured in every major periodical. Although Brown remained silent about the affair, Ronstadt had no qualms grumbling about the event and vented publicly for many months afterward.

Taking advantage of her celebrity power, Ronstadt had relationships with a large number of high-profile figures. Her romance with Jerry Brown, the Governor of California and presidential hopeful, gave her front page publicity throughout the world.

The final Linda Ronstadt album of the 1970s was issued in the fall of 1978. *Living In The USA* featured the attractive – now thirty-two year old – petite brunette wearing ultra-short satin hot pants and on roller skates. Demand for new product from her was so strong that the record had the highest advance sales figures of any album to date. More than 2.1 million copies were shipped to record stores nationwide. It knocked the ever popular *Grease* soundtrack out of #1 and was certified Double Platinum. The only down side was that *Living In The USA* came off as less inspired than her recent releases and received a mixed response from critics.

Still, the hit songs continued. 'Back In The USA', 'Just One Look', and 'Alison' were all issued on singles and climbed various charts. But the biggest hit from *Living In The USA* was a smolderingly soulful version of Smokey Robinson's classic 'Ooh Baby Baby'. To this day, Linda's version of the song stands as one of her finest moments. At the time, Disco

★ ★ ★

was at its peak and controlled the airwaves as well as popular culture everywhere. But Linda's interpretation of 'Ooh Baby Baby', which featured crackling alto sax work from David Sanborn, reached #2 at Easy Listening radio, climbed to #7 on *Billboard*'s Hot 100, and even crossed over to the Soul music chart. It was a rare feat for black radio stations to play non-black artists, but breaking new ground was now commonplace for the versatile vocalist.

Ronstadt made roller skating more fashionable in the late 1970s. Here is an image from her Living In The USA *photo shoot. The album had the biggest advance sales order of any album in history – shipping 2.1 million copies. It was her fourth multi-Platinum album in the second half of the Seventies alone.*

★ ★ ★

Ronstadt spent much of her time on the road, playing to huge audiences, throughout the 1970s and 1980s. Although she never enjoyed touring, she dutifully accepted it as part of her occupation. She is shown above at Michigan's Pine Knob in the summer of 1978.

In the 1970s, television, newspapers, and magazines were the public mediums of news and information. This was long before cable television, the Internet, and digital mayhem. *Playboy* magazine was one of – if not *the* – most widely circulated publication(s) in the world. An anticipated annual event was the spring announcement of the *Playboy Reader's Music Poll* results, with its colorful caricature images. Beginning in 1976, Linda Ronstadt was named the most popular female singer in both Rock and Country categories. She ranked #1 in both polls five consecutive years. (Eventually, in 1981, she would come in second to Pat Benatar in the Rock field.)

Many years before the Rock & Roll Hall of Fame was conceptualized, *Playboy* instituted its own Music Hall of Fame. Created to acknowledge original artists of lasting influence and significance, the magazine annually inducted the one artist who received the greatest number of votes. The first musician to receive induction was Jazz great Dave Brubeck. Through the

★ ★ ★

years Frank Sinatra, Ray Charles, Miles Davis, John Lennon, Mick Jagger, Jimi Hendrix, Eric Clapton, Elton John, and Stevie Wonder were among the music legends to hold the yearly spotlight. In 1978, the much deserved tribute went to Linda Ronstadt. The publication's essay would insightfully surmise,

> "Linda Ronstadt…is everyone's first love. She is always the girlfriend but never the roommate; the passionate pubescent but never the tail wager…Her own voice became the emotional cutting edge – a touchstone against which her listeners could measure their own angst. Linda's poignancy maps out the rather vacuous emotional terrain of the Seventies. She's there to add the humanness, the little girl lost-ness that reinforces our prevalent desperado myth and makes cowboys of us all. In the kingdom of the heartbroken, Linda Ronstadt is Queen, and a long reign seems assured."

Additionally, in 1980, in the same issue that published the annual music poll winners, Linda Ronstadt was the featured *Playboy* interview subject. She was characteristically candid.

As disclosed in Mark Bego's 1990 bio, Linda's personal revenue in 1978 was a phenomenal $12 million dollars. According to the US Bureau of Labor Statistics, that sum equated to 2014 dollars would amount to $43,489,693.00.

This figure was calculated using the CPI (Consumer Price Index), which rose 257% in thirty-six years. Often touted as "the highest paid woman in the music business", this computation was to be her standard income range for years to come. In 1987, Casey Kasem stated on his *American Top 40* radio show that her annual income in the Eighties was an average of "$10 million a year."

As the 1970s came to a close, Linda Ronstadt was, indeed, a hot commodity. She had become the biggest female recording artist in the music business – up to that point in time. (The Eighties would produce

Madonna and Whitney Houston as even more potent female superstars.) *Cash Box* magazine honored her with a special award as Female Artist of the Decade. Writer Vivian Claire, in her bio, *Linda Ronstadt*, referred to "the second half of the 1970s" as "the time when Linda Ronstadt's popularity began to rival baseball's (popularity)". She also observed that, "It's hard to believe that anyone dressed like she is can be so sexy." Claire summed up her subject as "one of the most compellingly sexual public figures since Marilyn Monroe."

Perhaps Mary Ellen Moore best analyzed it in her cover story on Linda in *Country Music People*, when she stated, "Linda Ronstadt is easily the most successful female Rock & Roll *and* Country star at this time." Moore went to state that,

> "Unlike other unfortunate cover girls, Linda's position as darling of the press is not a flash in the pan. She has not only been around for a long long time, but the way things look, she's going to be around for a lot longer."

Indeed, America was in the throes of Ronstadt fever as her fame and popularity reached an unparalleled altitude.

As it turned out, Linda wouldn't be the only Ronstadt sibling to relocate to Los Angeles in search of fame as a musician. In 1975, while in his early twenties, Michael Ronstadt left Arizona to make it as a musical discovery. At various times, he resided with his mega-star big sister in her Malibu beach house at 38 Malibu Colony Drive. However, after five years of playing area clubs, he had yet to achieve a recording contract or a successful breakthrough. In 1980, Mike returned to Tucson and took over the family hardware business. He and his wife, Deborah Jean, whom he'd known since his days at Catalina High, had two sons, Michael Gilbert and Peter Gilbert. (Today, in 2014, Mike and his sons tour the United States with their own sonic experience as Ronstadt Generations. They have even played the Detroit area.)

★ ★ ★

Linda entered the 1980s with a new look and image – as a Punk Rock artist. Her first album of the new decade was a post Punk/New Wave-styled record. She had had her hair cut extra short and spiky and toured in support of Mad Love, *her seventh million-selling album in five years.*

PUNK ROCK DIVA

Linda was growing restless and was looking for new forms of musical expression. As the Seventies came to an end, bands like the Police, Blondie, and the Clash were experiencing major breakouts. Their sound and style were reflective of Great Britain's Punk Rock movement. The Los Angeles and New York music scenes scrambled to emulate the energy and excitement that the United Kingdom was producing.

Linda became enthralled with this so-called New Wave movement. She spent much of 1979 checking out nightclubs where new American bands were honing their craft. One such group she discovered was the Cretones. She decided that this would be the sound for her next album and chose this thrashing, raw music to usher into the 1980s.

★ ★ ★

It was at the turn of the decade when Linda moved to a bigger and better dwelling. Her new abode was located a mere fifteen miles away, in exclusive Brentwood, at 241 North Rockingham Avenue. In a strange coincidence, she moved in across the street from 360 North Rockingham where celebrity football player/running back, O. J. Simpson, who was divorcing his current wife, Marguerite, resided with his teenage girlfriend, Nicole Brown. Linda and Nicole were very friendly during the nine years that Ronstadt lived in Brentwood, often walking their dogs together.

Getting a jump on the new decade, Linda Ronstadt released her first Punk-oriented single, 'How Do I Make You?', in January of 1980. Radio and music fans wasted no time in embracing her new approach. The song shot up the charts into the Top Ten. Perhaps the greatest surprise was Linda's new look. Her black hair was cropped ultra-short and spiky while she dressed in Punk fashions of black and pink. It was a daring move but it was only the beginning of some drastic career risk taking for the singer.

Linda Ronstadt punks out

★ ★ ★

Linda called her New Wave album *Mad Love*. One trademark element that wasn't greatly altered was the core subject matter of her music. It was a tougher sound and exterior for her but the central subject matter was still present. Her clear, affectionate voice actually growled on much of the material. *Mad Love* debuted at a record shattering #5 in its first week on the album chart. To no one's surprise this was a first for any female artist, corroborating her continued power in the Eighties.

A familiar theme – the pain of romance – was revisited for the record's second single release. 'Hurt So Bad' was a 1960s hit in two different versions, one by Little Anthony & the Imperials and the other by the Lettermen. The *Mad Love* version overflowed with scorching intensity that was absent in the two prior translations. The smash that Linda scored with 'Hurt So Bad' stands as the definitive version of the classic, in addition to being her highest debuting and fastest climbing song ever on the Hot 100. It would blast into the Top 10 in a mere six weeks. For the fourth time, in 1980, Ronstadt would be named *Billboard*'s #1 Female Artist of the Year.

In the spring of 1980, while Ronstadt toured America with her new band, which included Mark Goldenberg of the Cretones, *Mad Love* became her record seventh million-selling album in a row. (Her *Greatest Hits Volume 2*, released late that same year, was her eighth consecutive Platinum-certified album.) Even more amazingly, she accomplished this in just a little over five years. Her romance with the California Governor was still intact and he was now campaigning for President of the United States. Linda performed numerous benefit concerts to raise funds for Brown's campaign. Buttons with the caption 'Linda Ronstadt for First Lady' became a common spotting during this time as well. Women pinned them on their handbags while men wore them on their jackets.

★ ★ ★

Linda never lost touch with the kid inside of her. Her childhood served as a stimulus for much of her adult life. During a hectic 1980, she was a very special guest star on The Muppet Show. *She is shown here kissing Kermit The Frog.*

LINDA'S INFLUENCE AND IMPACT

Linda's influence on Rock & Roll inspired many other women, both in and out of the music business. During the 1970s and 1980s she was the biggest female concert draw in the world, with a median audience of twenty to thirty thousand live fans per show. Stevie Nicks and Pat Benatar are among those women who have acknowledged her influence on them, with Benatar gushing to *Rolling Stone* magazine in late 1980, "There are lots of great women singers around. How can I be the best? Ronstadt is still alive!"

Unpredictably, on the heels of her transition into a Punk Rock diva, Linda packed her bags and moved to New York City in the summer of 1980. She made yet another surprise career move when she starred

★ ★ ★

in Gilbert & Sullivan's century old Operetta, *The Pirates of Penzance*. Regarding her drastic metamorphosis, Linda recounted some two decades later for T. J. McGrath,

> "I hated it after a while. Rock singing just tears up your voice. It becomes an animal act or circus sideshow or sporting event as you travel through these stadium tube tunnels to get to your seat, and along the way your senses are assaulted by crass merchandizing ranging from bumper stickers to hot dogs. High arching guitar solos tend to dominate the conceived Rock show and everyone pulls out their lighters on cue. I really needed a change of pace…I had to do something different because it was getting so stale. So I went back to New York and tried to get into a smaller theatre."

For the first time in her life, she employed the services of a vocal coach – Marge Rivingston – to support her in training for the rigorous demands of singing in an operatic register. Following a successful run at the 1,800 seat Delacorte Theatre in Central Park, the musical moved to Broadway. According to the IBDB (Internet Broadway Data Base) website, *The Pirates of Penzance* ran from January to July of 1981 in the 1,900-plus seat Uris Theatre (renamed the Gershwin Theatre in 1983), in mid-town Manhattan. Ben Fong-Torres would later inscribe, "The show was a smash, and shortly after the summer run, it hit Broadway, where it won, among other honors, three Tony Awards (along with a nomination for Ronstadt as Best Actress)."

Looking back on Linda's initial foray into the operatic genre, T. J. McGrath would himself recall,

> "Crowds hoping to see the First Lady of Rock fall on her face were in for a shock. Not only was she able to keep up with the vocalists in the Opera, she was getting standing ovations for her singing."

★ ★ ★

At the start of the 1980s, Ronstadt undertook her first venture away from the world of Rock & Roll when she starred in the extended Broadway run - and later filmed the successful movie version - of The Pirates Of Penzance. *She harvested rave reviews for her performance and was even nominated for a Tony Award.*

As demanding as her schedule was, Linda still found time to get together with legendary record producer Jerry Wexler and record tracks for a proposed album of Jazz standards. Having grown up listening to the Great American Song Book, she had become preoccupied with the concept of recording a collection of the classic tunes. Her role in *Pirates* fueled the desire even more.

Unfortunately, what she and Jerry Wexler recorded was not up to her standards. Asylum Records was not keen on releasing what she and Wexler had come up with – for a number of reasons – during her stay in New York and the tracks were ultimately shelved. They would, however, surface in the new millennium as a popular bootleg.

★ ★ ★

★ ★ ★

6

Linda's Sonic Evolution

Although she had enjoyed a long ride as America's Rock Queen, as the Eighties wore on Linda Ronstadt found herself yearning to expand her professional abilities beyond the dominions of contemporary music. Shortly after completing her extended Broadway run in *The Pirates of Penzance*, in the summer of 1981, she commenced recording what would turn out to be her final Rock & Roll album, *Get Closer*.

Linda located the title track, which was written that year by Jon Carroll. She loved the energy and driving melody of the song and had no strain with its unusual 7/4 time signature. This would also mark her principal recording of compositions by the legendary songsmith Jimmy Webb. She had admired his elaborate composing talents for many years. Webb's work had included many veteran hits made famous by Country music star Glen Campbell. On *Get Closer* Ronstadt covered Webb's mournful yet sensual 'Easy For You To Say' and the ornate tune 'The Moon Is A Harsh Mistress'.

1981 was another non-stop year for the vigorous performer. In addition to her touted work on Broadway and in the studio, she undertook extensive tours of America, Canada, and Japan. It was also year of austere highs and lows for the Ronstadt family. Linda's brother, Peter, was elected Tucson, Arizona's Chief of Police. However, a personal tragedy also hit the Ronstadt clan when Ruth Mary was diagnosed with lung

★ ★ ★

cancer. Linda dealt with it by throwing herself deeply into her work. Late in the year she moved to London, England where she began filming the movie version of *The Pirates of Penzance*.

In 1982, Linda released her sensational Grammy Award winning Get Closer *album. It was one of her most exciting releases and would turn out to be her last disc in the Rock field. The accompanying music videos were a hit with MTV audiences. Her red and white polka dot dress became something of a fashion statement.*

Filming of the movie took several months and was a positive learning experience for Ronstadt. It taught her additional details about film making. Featured on the cover of *Home Video* magazine in 1983, Ben Fong-Torres noted, "Like any seasoned motion picture actor, Ronstadt was bored goofy between takes. In full Victorian getup, she could be spotted strumming an acoustic guitar or reading various works by Henry James."

Sadly, during the process, Ruth Mary's condition became increasingly grave. Development was rescheduled so that Linda could fly back to Tucson to spend some final moments with her mother. Shortly after her return to London, on March 4, 1982, Gilbert Ronstadt telephoned his youngest daughter to inform her that Ruth Mary had passed away. She was 67 years old.

★ ★ ★

Upon her return home to Los Angeles, assembly for *Get Closer* resumed. However, Ronstadt's infatuation with classic standards from the first half of the twentieth century continued. She had long been enamored with the arrangements of legendary band leader Nelson Riddle and longed to work with him. Peter Asher contacted Riddle via telephone that spring and he agreed to meet with Peter and Linda. She recalled for writer Barry Alfonso of Rhino,

> "We called Nelson, and I didn't know if he'd even heard of me...I think he knew who I was, vaguely. I doubt that he knew how I sang at all, nor would it have mattered, because whatever I sang on those (Rock) records didn't apply at all to what I did on the *What's New* record. It was a totally different voice."

Upon being granted a security clearance, he showed up one day at the Complex on Corinth Avenue where Linda was recording. He was immediately taken with not only her aptitude but with her initiative and sincerity.

Linda had initially hoped that Nelson would agree to arrange one or two songs for a future Jazz album. He explained to her that he never did single arrangements. He only did albums. Ronstadt was overjoyed when he consented to do an entire project with her. In fact, they wasted no time. After some brief rehearsals, they embarked on recording the tracks for what would eventually become the milestone *What's New* album. Sessions commenced in June before *Get Closer* was even completed.

ROCK & ROLL FINALE

The sessions for *Get Closer* wrapped in August of 1982. Even though she was more eager about her work with Nelson Riddle at the moment, Linda was obligated to spend the next year promoting her *Get Closer* album. The jamming title cut was released as the premier single a couple of weeks in advance of the album in September. It was accompanied by a colorful music video featuring Linda in the red and white polka dot dress

★ ★ ★

worn for the cover photographs. MTV, which had just completed its first year of operation, was catching on with television cable subscribers. It gave extensive play to the video while the song took off on CHR (Contemporary Hit Radio) and AOR (Album Oriented Rock) radio stations. Lamentably, the hugely popular weekly musical variety show, *Solid Gold*, tried to but was never able to secure Linda's appearance on the show. They did feature 'Get Closer' being lip synched by street pedestrians as a supplement though.

Ronstadt switched gears musically in 1983, releasing an album of Big Band Jazz tunes from the first half of the Twentieth Century. What's New *was a surprise smash, reaching the top of the* Billboard *album chart and selling nearly four million copies in the United States alone.*

Get Closer was certified Gold in November and would eventually move close to a million copies. In December, Ronstadt filmed three additional music videos – for 'Lies', 'Tell Him', and 'I Knew You When' – to promote the album. 'I Knew You When' was chosen as the follow up to 'Get Closer'. Early in 1983, it followed its predecessor up the Top 40.

Just as 'I Knew You When' reached its zenith, the movie version of *The Pirates of Penzance* was released to movie theatres nationwide. It was presented as a double feature with the Rolling Stones' robust *Let Spend The Night Together* concert film. Linda Ronstadt broke more new ground when *Pirates* became the first Pay-For-View cinematic effort in history. Cable television was taking off like a shot during this time and she was once again at the forefront of a pioneering movement. It was an exciting era, for sure, with Michael Jackson's *Thriller* album controlling the landscape on its way to becoming the biggest selling record – with an eventual 29 million US copies sold – in music history.

1983 also marked the momentous twenty-fifth anniversary of the recording industry's highest accolade, the Grammy Awards. Yet again, Linda found herself nominated in multiple categories. Her *Get Closer* album was up for Best Pop Vocal Performance Female, while the fiery song itself was nominated for Best Rock Vocal Performance Female. She had been invited to perform live on the Grammy telecast in the past but had turned down offers due to stage fright. To the delight of her fans, this was the year she finally agreed to do it. That evening she performed a stimulating presentation of her sweltering hit song wearing the now infamous polka dot dress. Even Grammy host John Denver was smitten with her, exclaiming, "She looks kinda nice in those polka dots, doesn't she?"

There were several predictions that she would walk away with one or both trophies that night, especially considering her now veteran standing in the industry, but she lost out to Melissa Manchester and Pat Benatar (who captured the Rock Female award for the third consecutive year). *Get Closer* did, however, win the Grammy for Best Album Package, given to John Kosh, the noted Art Director who had won in the same category in 1978 for designing Linda's erotic *Simple Dreams* album.

In March, the masses tuned in as Ronstadt appeared on *The Tonight Show with Johnny Carson* where she performed her signature 'Blue Bayou' – at Johnny's request – along with 'Get Closer' and 'Easy For You To Say'. She nervously flubbed the lyrics to the final song. Looking sensual in an ultra-short black dress and extra-high heels, she and Carson flirted and joked with each other. Drawing high ratings, he had her back on his program annually up until his retirement in the early Nineties.

Ronstadt hit the road shortly after *Get Closer* was released and toured again the following summer. 'Easy For You To Say' was one of her few

★ ★ ★

singles to fall short of the Top 40 but shot to #7 on the Adult Contemporary chart. Few people – if any – would have ever surmised that it would be her swan song as a Rock's foremost lady. Linda had many years of surprises in store and the public would witness the next in a plethora of career reinventions from her before the year was out.

BIG BAND JAZZ CHANTUESE

Upon completing an arduous nine months of recording sessions for *What's New* in the spring of 1983, Linda immediately hit the grueling concert trail for the duration of the summer, still promoting *Get Closer*. Without stopping to rest, she went straight into promoting *What's New* upon its September release. It served as quite a shock to most of her fan base. Gone was the electric guitar and drums based sound that had long been synonymous with her. In their place was a forty-seven piece Jazz orchestra performing a serene all-ballad presentation.

Bucking the industry trend of releasing an advance single to spur album sales, Ronstadt waited a month after *What's New*'s release to put out a single. She chose the dreamy title cut which was aided by an equally dreamy music video. The song took off rapidly at Jazz and Adult Contemporary radio stations, where it hit the Top Five in time for the holidays. (The next single, 'I've Got A Crush On You', did almost as well.) More surprising was its strong impact at Pop radio, in the process spending an amazing fourteen weeks in *Billboard*'s Hot 100 listing and breaking into the Top 40 in the *Cash Box* register.

What's New remains one of the biggest selling records in Linda's nearly fifty years a professional singer. By the end of the milestone year, 1983, *What's New* was the third biggest selling album in the country (behind *Thriller* and Lionel Richie's *Can't Slow Down*). It would go on to sell nearly four million copies in the States alone. Ronstadt and Riddle endorsed the album extensively, appearing all over network television and touring exhaustively. Not only did it expose young music fans to the sounds of a significant, bygone era, but it opened a flood gate of contemporary singers jumping on the bandwagon to record their own

★ ★ ★

'standards' albums.

It was a tremendous risk for Linda to take on a style and image completely foreign to what she was known for. However, her huge fan base was so strong that they welcomed the transformation with open arms. Big Band Jazz radio played her songs alongside Benny Goodman and the Dorsey brothers, proving her talent was so universal that she could adapt to any singing technique and succeed admirably with it.

Linda enlisted the legendary arranger and conductor Nelson Riddle for her What's New *album. It was such a rewarding experience that she created two more Platinum-selling Big Band Jazz albums,* Lush Life *and* For Sentimental Reasons, *with the maestro.*

Nearly two decades later, Linda would recapitulate for Barry Alfonso, a writer for Rhino Records/Entertainment, commemorating the twentieth anniversary of *What's New* which was now being issued on DVD Audio,

> "There was an enormous body of music that I loved that just wasn't being addressed in popular music...I think that in the second half of the twentieth century in American Pop music, we made great records, and in the first half of

★ ★ ★

the century, they wrote great songs. I was dying to sing songs that were beautifully written for singers, with lyrics that would talk about something other than a teenage love affair."

By 1983, Linda's personal worth was over $40 million dollars. She owned luxury homes in Malibu and Brentwood, California, as well as in Manhattan, New York. She was one of the most celebrated and advantaged celebrities in entertainment. As a result, she was wealthy beyond description. Although she had never married, she had been involved in innumerable relationships with scores of other celebrities. In 1983, she met a then-unknown aspiring comedian and actor named Jim Carrey. Interestingly, though she had dated mostly older men throughout her life, Carrey was sixteen years younger than Ronstadt. (She was 37 while he was just 21.) He moved into her Brentwood mansion and she hired him as her opening act on the *What's New* tour.

Linda explored the history of Jazz — and glamour as well — with her Big Band-styled albums. They displayed the singing superstar in a classy setting

The May-December romance between Ronstadt and Carrey lasted for only several months during mid-1983. Not long after they went their separate ways, Linda became involved romantically with noted director and filmmaker George Lucas. Both stars went to great lengths to keep their romance quiet. To their credit, they managed to avoid paparazzi and gossip columns almost completely during the next five years. In a 1984 *People* magazine cover story on Linda, it was revealed that,

> "Ronstadt, 38, and Lucas, 39, have never been photo-graphed together. But they have been together often since a friend introduced them in December. She's a frequent visitor to San Anselmo (California), where Lucas lives, and his Skywalker Ranch, a nearby sequestered enclave for filmmaking...He has visited her Malibu and Brent-wood homes."

The twenty-sixth annual Grammy Award nominations saw Ron-stadt's *What's New* album up against some formidable competition for Best Pop Vocal Performance Female. Competing for the coveted award were Donna Summer's 'She Works Hard For The Money', Bonnie Tyler's 'Total Eclipse Of The Heart', Sheena Easton's 'Telephone', and Irene Cara's 'Flashdance What A Feeling'.

In what was the most anticipated and most widely viewed Grammy telecast in history – a record it still holds as of 2014 – all five women performed live that evening. It was *fait accompli* that Michael Jackson walked away with a record-setting eight Grammys but when Irene Cara pulled off the ostensibly impossible event of winning the Pop Female award, *Variety*, and many other reports fumed, claiming it to be "the evening's biggest upset!" Every pundit in the entertainment business had forecasted *What's New* to be the conclusive winner. Even Cara was caught totally off guard, expecting Linda Ronstadt to be on stage accept-ing the trophy that night.

1984 was another whirlwind year for her as she toured the globe with Nelson, who became a second father to Linda, starred on Broadway again (as Mimi in Puccini's full-fledged Opera *La Boheme*), and recorded her second album of Jazz standards entitled *Lush Life*. It was a natural move to create a follow-up with Riddle again conducting his orchestra. After

★ ★ ★

finishing their summer tour, they committed their sophomore effort to tape.

MORE JAZZ – AND SWING

Lush Life was far more varied and flowing than *What's New* in its material and arrangements. Instead of lone ballads it featured several Swing tunes that included a 1930 German composition titled 'Ich Bin Von Kopf Bis Fub Auf Liebe Eingestellt' by Friedrich Hollander. It was originally sung by Marlene Dietrich in *Der Blue Engel*, directed by Josef von Sternberg, that same year. Translated to English, it decoded to 'Falling In Love Again'.

In addition, Riddle and Ronstadt recorded the upbeat 'Can't We Be Friends?' and Rodgers & Hart's bouncy 'You Took Advange Of Me'. They employed the services of Toni Basil to choreograph and direct an amusing music video for 'You Took Advantage Of Me'. Basil had recently scored a Platinum-selling #1 hit with her song 'Mickey'. Having remained on positive terms with Jim Carrey, he was cast as the wolf in Linda's video.

The other video created for the *Lush Life* project was for the transcendent version of Hoagy Carmichael and Johnny Mercer's 'Skylark'. It had a rich history dating back to 1941. Mercer spent a year toiling with the lyrics, which were about his then-sweetheart Judy Garland. 'Skylark' also inspired the Buick automobile of the same name. Linda scored a sizable hit on Jazz and A/C radio, again just in time for Christmas, in 1984, stopping just short of the Top 10. Likewise, *Lush Life* was one of the hottest selling products of the Christmas season, going Platinum in only a few short weeks.

Another notable facet of the album was its stellar packaging. Imitating a 1940s scenario, it featured her in elegant attire with the two full-size Airedale Terriers that were shown in the 'Skylark' music video. The album cover was designed as a deluxe hat box with a removable top. It was an appropriately classy look and would become the third Linda Ronstadt album to win the Grammy for Best Album Package.

Touring with nearly fifty seasoned Jazz musicians during the

★ ★ ★

mid-Eighties was a far cry from touring with a group of rowdy Rock & Rollers. At home in Los Angeles she had the services of Chuck Norton, a professional fitness trainer. In nearly every city the band played, Linda would locate a gym where she could work out.

It had been fascinating to view her physical transformation over the years. Linda had been the free-spirited epitome of the Bohemian-type hippie chick in the late 1960s and well into the 1970s. As her fame grew, she continued to exhibit a sexy image but gradually became more conservative. By this point in time her likeness had taken on a genuine sophistication.

Concurrent with her latest album was Ronstadt's return to 'the great white way' in Giacomo Puccini's *La Boheme,* an Opera that dated back to 1896. Her success in *The Pirates Of Penzance* had boosted her confidence level and she felt capable of mastering a starring role in a full-fledged Opera.

The site of this theatrical event was considerably smaller than her previous operatic endeavors. Unfortunately, most critics and theatre goers were less than impressed with her portrayal of Mimi and the play had a short run. Held at the 275 seat Anspacher Theatre, the production opened on November 29 and closed on New Year's Eve. Nevertheless, Linda once again had expanded her vocal and acting skills even further.

As 1985 opened, everything in her life was stable and rolling along. Sadly, though, it would be another year integrated with tragedy and grief. Nelson Riddle had been suffering from a serious liver disease and his health would decline steadily throughout the year. Due to his failing physical condition, he was unable to maintain the pace he'd been moving at.

That summer, Linda and Nelson returned to the Complex for the recording of their third and – as it turned out – final collaboration together. Initially planned as a double-album set, the sessions ultimately became a race against time. Linda became increasingly concerned as she watched her mentor become thinner and weaker. They had developed a close father and daughter-like bond in the past three years. Still, she was complacent with the evolution that her work with the maestro had generated. She explicated to Alfonso,

"In Rock & Roll, we're all supposed to stand there and try to look hip and tough, and I was tired of that. So this was a more reasonable voice and attitude. I think this is my most authentic voice, and finally it came out."

The final curtain fell on October 6, 1985 when Nelson Smock Riddle Jr. died at Cedar-Sanai Hospital in West Hollywood. He was 64 years old. Linda was devastated and found speaking at his funeral service very hard to do. She spent the rest of the year quietly mourning her lost mentor and friend.

At the twenty-eighth annual Grammy Award ceremonies, held in early 1986, special attention was given to both Linda Ronstadt and Nelson Riddle, who were each nominees. Before the telecast went on the air, Mr. Riddle was posthumously awarded Best Instrumental Arrangement Accompanying A Vocal for the 'Lush Life' track. (At a Lansing, Michigan concert engagement, in 2003, Linda pronounced the song to be her "absolute favorite standard of all time, without a doubt.")

After sorrowfully accepting the Grammy on Nelson's behalf, Linda – and her old colleague James Taylor – presented the first televised award of the evening to Phil Collins who greeted her with a kiss. Miss Ronstadt looked stunning as Michael Jackson and Elizabeth Taylor, along with the who's who of the music world in the audience, watched from the front row. Moments later, Dionne Warwick and Julian Lennon would announce the Pop Vocal Female honors. *Lush Life* had been universally considered the front runner in a superstar line-up of Linda Ronstadt, Madonna, Tina Turner, Pat Benatar, and, the surprise victor, newcomer Whitney Houston.

Ronstadt's exciting career had reached a plane on a very illustrious plateau. She continued to be one of the most lauded and successful artists in the business, revered by critics and music lovers alike. Better yet, her shining icon status would maintain for many years to come.

A TANTALIZING TRIO

In January of 1986, Ronstadt reconvened with her long time friends

Dolly Parton and Emmy Lou Harris in another attempt at putting together a long delayed 'trio' album. Their prior endeavors as a recording threesome were thwarted as label executives, managers, and producers interfered and tried to control the three diverse women singers. Ultimately, this time they created a unanimously praised album that would sell millions.

The camaraderie of Linda's friendship with Dolly and Emmy dated back to around 1975 when all three *ingénues* were taking off in their own careers. In early 1976, the three appeared together on the syndicated television series *Dolly*. They each had individual looks, sounds, and styles but the contrast they created collectively was very appealing. One of the most noteworthy cuts to appear from previous recordings was the Dolly-penned 'My Blue Tears' which came out on *Get Closer*.

It was now a full decade since their first television appearance together. They were now fully confident, decision making, mature superstars. One of the first – albeit offbeat – song choices they made was to record the #1 Pop hit from 1958 'To Know Him Is To Love Him'. They would spend the better part of 1986 working on the elevens tracks that would be the landmark *Trio* album.

The release of the elegant multi-million selling, Grammy Award winning Trio *album was a landmark. It reestablished Ronstadt strongly with Country music audiences. Linda, Dolly, and Emmy Lou are pictured here in 1987.*

★ ★ ★

7

Movies, Mariachi, and More

As Linda celebrated her fortieth birthday, in July of 1986, she signed on for additional projects in what would be one of the busiest years of her life. She brought in her old friend James Taylor to help her complete the arrangements for her final album with the now deceased Nelson Riddle. Her record company and management also loaned her out to MCA for the soundtrack of what would be the highest grossing non-Disney animated film to date. It would be titled *An American Tail*.

Furthermore, she joined a cast of heralded musicians that included Keith Richards, Eric Clapton, and Robert Cray, on the eighteenth of October, 1986, to perform an electrifying version of 'Back In The USA' in honor of Chuck Berry's sixtieth birthday. The performance took place at the 4,000-plus seat Fox Theatre in St. Louis, Missouri and was included in the documentary, *Hail! Hail! Rock & Roll*, which ran on the big screen in movie theatres throughout the autumn of 1987.

RONSTADT RETURNS TO THE MOVIES

The plot of *An American Tail* revolves around Fievel Mousekewitz and his Jewish family of mice who emigrate from Russia to America in the year 1885, following the abolition of their village by cats. Directed by Don Bluth and produced by Sullivan Bluth Studios and Amblin Enter-

★ ★ ★

tainment, *An American Tail* was released during Thanksgiving week and would gross an astounding $47 million in the US and $84 million globally.

The movie's theme song, 'Somewhere Out There', was written by the experienced team of Barry Mann and Cynthia Weil along with James Horner. After seeking out Linda Ronstadt and securing her involvement in the assignment, Linda was asked who she would like to duet with. R&B crooner James Ingram was reportedly at the top of her list and jumped at the chance to record with the legendary songstress.

The evolution of 'Somewhere Out There' came at a critical juncture in Ronstadt's career. After many years as contemporary music's premiere female artist, since 1983 she had transformed herself into a retro Jazz vocalist. The Pop world continued to evolve, becoming more electronic-based in the age of Madonna. It was becoming a question as to how viable forty year olds in the business were to the CHR (Contemporary Hit Radio) audience so besotted with Madonna and the current wave of MTV acts.

The final production of the tune would strongly reestablish Linda as a modern hit maker, becoming one of the biggest hits of her entire career as well as an enduring classic. 'Somewhere Out There' is a romantic and passionate recording, displaying the two renowned vocalists in peak form. The track is so spectacularly beautiful that instantly stops the listener in their tracks. Nearly three decades afterward, it remains a popular wedding song.

In 1987, Linda Ronstadt returned to the top of the Billboard Hot 100 *in a duet with smooth-voiced crooner James Ingram. The desirous song 'Somewhere Out There' was the theme from the smash animated movie* An American Tail. *Linda and James sang their hit live at a Fourth of July concert for Vietnam veterans.*

★ ★ ★

Released to radio in October, it received an immediate response from 'light' radio formats including the night time program *Pillow Talk*. Requests for the cut elevated quickly as it took off at A/C radio but wasn't breaking at Pop stations. Even following the film's release in November, it had yet to make *Billboard*'s Hot 100 (*Billboard* had eliminated the Bubbling Under chart in 1985.). By mid-December, the song's future looked bleak. According to industry beliefs at the time – and given the traditional method of promotion – if a record hadn't broken out in most major markets within six weeks, it was in jeopardy. In eight weeks, it could be considered dead in the water.

The tide finally turned when MTV picked up the heart-wrenching music video. As 1986 came to a close, 'Somewhere Out There' blasted up the Pop charts. Several weeks into the new year, it retuned Linda to the Top 40. It bulleted up the listings and in March it was the most popular song in America. Both the movie and the single became hugely popular throughout the world. In England, it gave Ronstadt her first Top 10 hit after twenty years in the business. Still the only format available at the time, it became one of the last 45 RPM vinyl singles to sell over a million copies, earning the duo a Gold-certified record from the RIAA.

Concurrent with 'Somewhere Out There' and the *American Tail* cinematic venture was Linda's third album of Big Band Jazz. Released almost exactly one year after the death of Nelson Riddle, *For Sentimental Reasons* was a fitting tribute to the departed maestro. Continuing in the same vein as *What's New* and *Lush Life*, it contained a similar mix of classics from the Twenties, Thirties, and Forties.

The most palpable song on the disc was Ronstadt's wistful yet buoyant interpretation of 'When You Wish Upon A Star'. Considered by many to be the best reading ever recorded of the classic, the 1940 Walt Disney adaption for *Pinocchio* was released on a single. It simultaneously climbed the Adult Contemporary chart with 'Somewhere Out There' and reached #32 at year's end.

Meanwhile, *For Sentimental Reasons* spent over six months on *Billboard*'s album chart, getting as high as #46. It went on to sell well over a million copies in the United States, earning the team of Ronstadt and

★ ★ ★

Riddle their third Platinum-certified album in a row. Even though Linda was sad about the loss of her beloved mentor, she found gratification in the work they did together. She continued to perform their songs for the rest of her performing years.

Without even waiting for the dust from the album to settle – and with 'Somewhere Out There' still at the top of the charts – Ronstadt launched yet another groundbreaking sonic venture. Her perpetually delayed collaboration with her singing sisters Dolly Parton and Emmy Lou Harris, *Trio*, was released in March of 1987. It quickly became the #1 Country album in the US while the advance single release of 'To Know Him Is To Love Him' climbed to #1 on the Country Songs chart. The album was a smash with Pop audiences as well and rapidly broke into the Top Ten of *Billboard*'s main album chart. It would be one of the biggest selling Country albums to date – prior to the huge Country music boom led by Garth Brooks in the Nineties – selling several million in the United States alone.

Flourishing singles and popular music videos continued unabated from the album. 'Telling Me Lies', 'Those Memories Of You', and 'Wildflowers' were all Top 10 Country hits. The album would receive nominations in several Grammy categories including a bid for the cherished top award of Album Of The Year alongside Michael Jackson, Whitney Houston, Prince, and U2.

As the Eighties neared a close, Ronstadt had long become frustrated and disillusioned with the Los Angeles region and the superficial attitudes of celebrity. After much scouting, she had developed a fascination with the San Francisco community and, in early 1988, purchased an elaborate multi-million dollar home in the exclusive Pacific Heights district. Choosing the environment as a more normal place to reside, she established the Golden Gate City as her new habitation.

Her new mansion was elaborate nearly beyond description. Prior to moving in, Linda had it completely remodeled to her specifications. In addition to its seven bedrooms, the four level manor had a private office, an *au pair* suite, a music room, a play room, a powder room, seven fireplaces, five full baths, two half baths, a dumbwaiter, stained glass windows and

★ ★ ★

chandeliers throughout. The spacious backyard featured an intricate play-house for her kids.

Linda relocated to San Francisco in the late 1980s upon tiring of the Los Angeles community. This is the multi-million dollar house on Jackson Street that she owned until 1997. Although she moved back to Tucson for some time, she would return to live in the Golden Gate City in the Twenty-First Century.

Asked about the reason behind her move up north, Ronstadt responded to a reporter in *The San Francisco Examiner*, "I like the architecture and I like that people don't occupy ninety percent of their thinking with whether they have the right haircut, or the right outfit, or whether their plastic surgery is up to date. I find that mentality exhausting."

A ROCKER RETURNS TO HER ROOTS

The world of music surrounded Linda Ronstadt while she was grow-ing up in the Grand Canyon State. She was enveloped in an endless array of sonic genres. Having learned the music of Mariachi from her paternal Mexican grandparents, it was passed down to her as an integral facet of her heritage. Accordingly, it would remain her biggest influence throughout her life.

Many times Linda had discussed the prospect of recording such a disc of this rich cultural art form with the representatives of her record com-pany. Even given her superior position in the music industry, the con-cept was repeatedly rejected. Asylum Records executives simply couldn't fathom the reality of such a recording being viable.

As far back as 1977, she had been anxious to record in Spanish. Releasing a Spanish-language version of 'Blue Bayou', translated to 'Lago

★ ★ ★

Azul', was perhaps the first major step in that direction. Linda would often intersperse some Spanish phrasing into her live performances of the venerable song. She recalled for Craig Rosen, in his *Billboard Book of Number One Albums:*

> "I was trying to sound like a Mexican singer with that fal-setto thing at the end. I really wanted to do a traditional Mexican record, but I couldn't. The record company really didn't want me to, and (my) band didn't know how play it. We were on the road all the time, so I couldn't find some way to get off the bus and go down to Mexico and find a band to help me do it."

Nevertheless, Linda continued to research every detail of the historic traditions and learned every nuance of the complex singing technique. The beautiful and legendary Mexican torch singer Lola Beltran had forever served as her muse and her inspiration.

Upon completion of the *Trio* project, Ronstadt was adamant that her next career undertaking would in fact be an album of traditional Mariachi songs. Ever the astute musicologist, Linda enlisted the world's most qualified musicians to accompany her in her latest endeavor.

As she relayed to a live, televised audience in 2008, "I told (my record company) that I had given them years of commercial recordings and I felt that I had, at last, earned this chance to indulge myself."

To say that *Canciones De Mi Padre* was a surprise hit would be a tremendous understatement. Released at the end of 1987, it sold like no other non-English language record ever had. It was certified Gold within just a few weeks. Linda promoted the album tirelessly, touring throughout the biosphere in an extravaganza that put many Broadway constructions to shame. It would go on to win Linda her fourth Grammy Award in the category of Best Mexican-American Performance.

It didn't stop there either. *Canciones De Mi Padre* did, in fact, return its creator to the Broadway stage. It was filmed for repeated cable broadcast as a live production. When Elektra Entertainment developed a video division, the show was released on video cassette and later on DVD. It introduced

★ ★ ★

the history of Mariachi to music fans worldwide. All told, the album sold well over two million copies in the United States alone – receiving Double Platinum certification – and establishing *Canciones De Mi Padre* as "the biggest selling non-English language album in record history."

In the late 1980s, Linda Ronstadt scored yet another musical triumph when she recorded Canciones De Mi Padre, *an album of traditional Mariachi compositions. To promote the disc, she toured internationally in an exquisite stage extravaganza.* Canciones De Mi Padre *became the biggest-selling non-English record in history.* The album eventually sold close to 10 million copies throughout the world.

Linda toured internationally in an effort to bring this cultural expedition to the public. She even took the show to Las Vegas even though she has always been outspoken in her disdain for Sin City, describing it as having "the pushiest, nastiest people."

In the 1980s, Linda developed some notoriety for being pushy and quite difficult at times. Accounts circulated regarding her contempt for her public and surliness toward people during appearances in concert and on television. Looking back on this time, in 2004 she grumbled to Mike Weatherford in the *Las Vegas Review Journal,*

"My backstage is closed. I don't want people around if they're not in the show. They wanted me to take a pho-

★ ★ ★

tograph with the owner (of the Aladdin Hotel), who was busy gambling away his family fortune…I'm not a picture pony. (Ginji Yasuda) got really mad because he was supposed to deliver this for the boss. I wound up having him thrown out. He got very belligerent and very rude, and we got very rude back."

TEAMING UP WITH A NEVILLE BROTHER

Ronstadt had long been an admirer of the Neville Brothers, a four sibling band from New Orleans, Louisiana. Their lead singer, Aaron, sang in a spectacularly impassioned falsetto. Linda often described him as having "the voice of an arch angel". As a solo, he had topped the Pop and R&B charts back in 1967 with the iridescent 'Tell It Like It Is'. However, despite the brothers' acclaim within the industry and a modest following, they had never found consistent commercial success.

The seeds of *Cry Like A Rainstorm-Howl Like The Wind* were sown during the summer of 1984. Ronstadt was on tour with her Jazz band entourage. During their stop in the Big Easy, she decided to go out and see the Neville Brothers live. She was caught off guard when Aaron Neville invited her up on stage to participate in a Doo-Wop medley. Later finding out that Aaron was a big fan of hers, she decided to ask him if he would record a future album with her. As she would claim in upcoming interviews, "It took me a year to work up the nerve to ask him to sing with me." However, she had so many demands on her that it would be five years before the opportunity arose to work with Aaron.

Cry Like A Rainstorm-Howl Like The Wind turned out to be a return to a more mainstream Pop/Rock sound for Linda Ronstadt. Recorded with an elaborate orchestra, it was filled mostly with sentimental – sometimes achingly painful – ballads of lost love. She revisited the catalogues of her old songwriter friends, Jimmy Webb and Karla Bonoff, for this recording. The closing cut, Bonoff's 'Goodbye My Friend', a song she wrote about losing a friend to AIDS, is heartbreaking to the point of distress.

The *Rainstorm* album was released in early October. It was immediately

★ ★ ★

certified Gold and by year's end it was Platinum. It went on to become one of the three highest selling recordings of Linda's entire career (along with *Simple Dreams* and *What's New*), earning Triple Platinum certification in America. It was also popular in many other regions of the world, earning many other Gold and Platinum awards.

What catapulted the record into orbit were in fact the duets with Neville. Although the album itself was far more adult-oriented than what radio was playing at the turn of the new decade, the pre-release single, 'Don't Know Much' was an immediate success. One of the most romantic songs ever recorded, radio stations pounced on it from day one. In an age of hair band Metal and electronic Dance music, 'Don't Know Much' beguiled radio listeners. Demand for the track was phenomenal. In its fifth week out, it was the #1 Adult Contemporary song in America (where it held for five straight weeks). Seemingly the only song on Pop radio not recorded with electronic synthesizers, it blasted up the Pop charts. In the final week of the 1980s, it was the most popular song in the country.

Linda continued to win Grammy Awards throughout the 1990s and into the Twenty-First Century. Two of them were for long-running #1 hit duets – 'Don't Know Much' and 'All My Life' – sung with New Orleans legend Aaron Neville.

★ ★ ★

"Don't Know Much" became a global happening, topping the charts in America, Canada, Europe, and throughout the world. 1989 was the year that the two song cassette became the new 'single' format and caused sales to skyrocket. "Don't Know Much" earned a Gold-certified record for the passionate duo of Linda Ronstadt and Aaron Neville.

Also during 1989, Linda's romance with filmmaker George Lucas ran its course after a five year courtship. While she was in New Orleans recording tracks for her *Rainstorm* album, she met impresario Quint Davis. Davis was, among other things, the owner of the New Orleans Jazz & Heritage Festival. There were immediate sparks between the two and they entered into a heavy romance. In the autumn of 1990, it was revealed in Mitchell Fink's People magazine column, *The Insider,* that the couple was engaged and planning a wedding in Cuernavaca, Mexico over the holidays. Various wire services picked up the news story and ran with it. Linda and Quint were together for several years but no wedding ever took place.

★ ★ ★

8

Parenthood and the Nineties

For many years, Linda had longed to be a mother and find a method of slowing down the hectic pace of her life. Even so, her incredibly high-powered career had kept her in constant motion for decades. In reality, in 1990, Linda was truly at an all time occupational peak.

At the thirty-second annual Grammy Awards, 'Don't Know Much' was nominated for Song Of The Year and Best Pop Performance By a Duo Or Group. Meanwhile, *Cry Like A Rainstorm-Howl Like The Wind* earned Linda yet another nomination in the Best Pop Vocal Performance Female category. Ronstadt and Neville performed live on the broadcast and proceeded to win in the Pop Duo or Group Performance field. This marked her fifth Grammy victory and his second. (They were so popular as a duo that they won in the identical category again the next year.)

'Don't Know Much' lit off another string of Pop and Adult Contemporary hits for Linda. She would experience a tremendous resurgence in radio – and music video channel – airplay during 1990. Shortly after their Grammy conquest, Linda Ronstadt and Aaron Neville were again #1 at A/C radio and at #11 on the Hot 100 – just one notch short of the Top Ten.

The Ronstadt/Neville team was so hot that, in April, a third duet, 'When Something Is Wrong With My Baby', was released. It was accompanied by another sensuous music video of the pair, with vignettes of Louisiana street scenes interspersed with the twosome in a New

★ ★ ★

Orleans nightclub. The song followed 'Don't Know Much' and 'All My Life' into the Top Five of the A/C charts and also climbed the Hot 100. Radio programmers and the public couldn't get enough of the superb duo. Aaron Neville was now at his career peak, becoming a millionaire as he approached the age of fifty.

Having already toured the European continent the previous autumn, Linda and Aaron spent the summer of 1990 touring major venues across the United States with the Neville Brothers as their opening act. It was a change of pace for Aaron who was accustomed to playing clubs and smaller venues. As the summer wound down, they made their way to Michigan's most famous concert site, Pine Knob. Shortly afterward, Ronstadt returned to California and Neville to his native Louisiana.

A NEW MOM AT FORTY-FOUR

There were changes in store for Miss Ronstadt as she entered into proceedings to adopt her first child. That Christmas holiday was a dream come true when, at the age of forty-four, she became a single parent to a newborn baby girl. She chose the name of Mary Clementine, which reflected her everlasting taste in the traditional and old-fashioned. There were no official announcements. When the news broke in 1991, Ronstadt was quoted in Mitchell Fink's column as claiming, "(The adoption) was a personal matter, and I never discuss my (private) life in public."

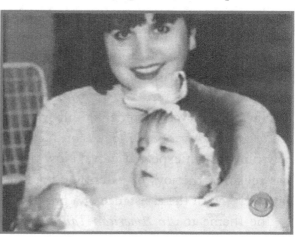

While residing in San Francisco, Linda Ronstadt adopted a baby girl at the end of 1990 and embraced single parenthood. She named her daughter Mary Clementine.

★ ★ ★

Following the outstanding success of her *Rainstorm* album, Linda began laying tracks for a proposed follow-up in similar stratum. The added responsibilities of caring for a new infant was added pressure for the star and her patience often grew short. After numerous attempts at recording another contemporary outing, it was obviously not coming together and set aside. The time had come for her to make more changes. As reported in *People*, and other publications, after nearly twenty years of producing her, Peter Asher stepped down from his production duties. He did, however, stay on board in his management capacity.

Ronstadt instead turned back to her ethnic roots for another collection of classic Mariachi recordings. Again enlisting Ruben Fuentes, she set about putting down tracks for *Mas Canciones (More Songs)* to be her first new release of the Nineties. Also largely integrated into the latest venture were Linda's brothers, Peter – who was retiring as Tucson's Police chief – and Mike.

Mas Canciones turned out to be nearly identical to the massively popular *Canciones De Mi Padre* in tone, content, and execution but it continued the opulent cultural traditional of its predecessor. More than any other recordings released in her life span, Linda considers these two albums to be the most emblematic of her existence.

Linda built a familiar strategy for the Christmas season of 1991. In addition to the release of her new Latin album, the year would mark her major return to the cinematic world in two separate components.

She would sign on – again with MCA – to record the sentimental theme for the continuing animated saga of Fievel Mousekewitz in *An American Tail-Fievel Goes West*. A bigger surprise to her fans was Linda Ronstadt's return to acting in front of the movie cameras for the holiday themed motion picture *La Pastorela*.

Having achieved an indelible hit with 'Somewhere Out There' from the original *American Tail* epic, contracting Linda's involvement for the new film was an expected move. Now the mother of an infant girl, she was relishing the joys of parenthood as she took her baby out on tour with her – with the assistance of a professional nanny.

The theme to *An American Tail-Fievel Goes West* was composed by

★ ★ ★

James Horner and Will Jennings. Entitled 'Dreams To Dream' it was released in the now current cassette single only format in late 1991. It did well at Adult Contemporary radio, reaching #13. But Linda's reign at Contemporary Hit Radio was spinning itself out as the aggressive trends of the Grunge movement and a newer electronic Dance music permeated the Pop music world in the 1990s.

The massive success of the *Cry Like A Rainstorm* album and tour had propelled Aaron Neville into the long deserved position of being a major artist. Linda produced his 1991 breakout Platinum album, *Warm Your Heart*. The lead single, a quixotic remake of 'Everybody Plays The Fool', hit #1 on *Billboard*'s Adult Contemporary chart and was a Top Ten Pop hit, too. Aaron scored three additional million-selling albums in the 1990s. His friendship with Linda continues unabated to the current day.

1991 was also the year that famed movie director Luis Valdez, best known for the 1987 cinematic blockbuster *La Bamba*, created *La Pastorela (The Shepherd's Tale)*. Valdez continued his Spanish-themed subject matter with *La Pastorela*. The plot concerns a group of raggedy shepherds on a pilgrimage to the Holy Land in search of the baby Jesus. One of the main characters in the film is San Miguel, an angel who repeatedly flies down from the heavens to rescue the pack from evil.

In 1991, Ronstadt returned to the cinematic world when she starred in La Pastorela. *Although admittedly not enthralled with movie making, Linda enjoyed the experience of this project and garnered positive reviews for her acting performance.*

★ ★ ★

Valdez was confident from the start that Linda Ronstadt would be ideal for the role of San Miguel. He excitedly approached her with an offer to star in his latest venture. Although she had some hesitation about returning to acting and movie making, she was captivated by the script. She was also strongly in favor of further promotion of her Hispanic ethnicity. Her schedule was frenetic but she was willing to sign on for it.

Linda's performance in *La Pasorela* was surprisingly strong and confident, garnering positive reviews. It was originally aired in December on PBS, the Public Broadcasting Service, and achieved high ratings. Although she declined to accept further offers for acting roles, the response that Ronstadt received for her role in the film served as a source of pride to her.

Also released just in time for the 1991 Christmas season was *Mas Canciones*. Virtually indistinguishable from *Canciones De Mi Padre*, the album further exposed the United States – and the rest of the globe – to the historic tradition of Mariachi. Though the performances were on a par with its forerunner, it seemed that *Canciones De Mi Padre* had amply covered the material. Not judging it by customary commercial standards, *Mas Canciones* eventually sold approximately 400,000 copies in the United States which was outstanding for a foreign language excursion.

At this point in Ronstadt's career, she had proven that she could thrive artistically, as well as commercially, with anything and everything she attempted. Accordingly, her record company was now far more inclined to indulge her ambitions. Choosing to keep her next contemporary recording on the back burner, she delved into yet another aspect of Spanish traditions.

Attempting a mission of Afro Cuban mores, she recorded *Frenesi (Frenzy)* during the following year. Released in September, and accompanied by a promotional appearance on *The Tonight Show*, with its brand new host Jay Leno, Linda's *Frenesi* album logged a single week on the *Billboard* album chart. It peaked at #193.

Whereas Linda still had the desire to continue recording – and touring – en *Espanol,* Elektra Entertainment was anxious to have their fabled songbird return to the English language. The company was secure in the

★ ★ ★

notion that their foremost female artist had more *tour de force* recordings in her future. Ronstadt was now moving into her late forties.

EXPLORING NEW AGE MUSIC

With this in mind, the recording of the masterpiece *Winter Light* commenced. Filled with ultra-sensitive interpretations of compositions from classic songwriters – from Burt Bacharach to Carole King to Anna McGarrigle – *Winter Light* would be one of the finest albums in a career that had now spanned nearly thirty years. Still sufficed with her trademark energy and drive, in 1993, while still touring heavily, she completed the tracks from June to September at the Site in Marin County, California. Now sans the venerable Peter Asher, Ronstadt produced the album herself with assistance from George Massenburg.

Just prior to *Winter Light*'s official release, in November of 1993, Linda embarked on a promotional tour of radio stations throughout the country. Discussing and plugging the New Age-styled material with prominent disc jockeys while jetting from city to city, she was anxious to wrap things up before another treacherous American winter set in. Her Detroit-area stop was at Dearborn's WNIC with Jim Harper as the host.

When the *Winter Light* album dropped, it reaped some of the strongest critical praise of her career. Linda herself had composed the ethereal title track, sung in a startling operatic range, for the movie *The Secret Garden*. *Billboard* magazine printed a full two-page ad to promote the disc, stating in part, "No matter what kind of song Linda Ronstadt chooses to sing, the light she shines on each is always the most brilliant and beautiful. Her *Winter Light* is the brightest yet."

Conversely, the record encountered a surprisingly modest reaction in sales and airplay. In spite of the substantial promotion, it peaked at #92 on *Billboard*'s album chart during a record healthy economy with a now pinnacle record industry. The album's first single release, the luxurious 'Heartbeats Accelerating', was even aided by a sumptuous music video. Nevertheless, the brilliant song topped off at #31 on A/C radio and only

★ ★ ★

'Bubbled Under' to #112. A second track, 'Oh No, Not My Baby' was later picked up by A/C stations but only reached #35.

Despite the tepid response, executives at Elektra were happy with the record, recognizing its creative prowess. Likewise, the artist was undaunted by her first 'commercial failure' in over two decades. It was now 1994 and as Linda Ronstadt rolled along with her career and life, she set about adding to her family. Adopting a baby boy who had been born in January, the new arrival was given the name Carlos Sangria Ronstadt. Linda claimed to have found contentment as a single mom.

Simultaneously, she reunited with Dolly and Emmy Lou to prepare a follow-up to their ground-breaking *Trio* project. The ladies set about choosing songs and working out arrangements for another anticipated release. But this time around something unexpected occurred. There was a major falling out between the benevolent Dolly and the direct and dominating Linda. The remaining trio member aligned herself with Linda.

There was no new Linda Ronstadt album in 1994. Dolly's vocals were reportedly "scrapped" – although they may simply have been shelved. What followed was an exchange of invective where both women gave interviews in which they hurled insults at each other in widely circulated periodicals.

Linda's demeanor through the years evolved in a more bellicose direction. She was, it seemed, quite set in her ways by middle age. She had thrown a volatile tantrum, blowing up at a *Rolling Stone* journalist who interviewed Ronstadt in her home at 2544 Jackson Street in early 1994. She was consistently rude and insolent to fans and the working public. Now she was about to prompt more bad publicity during her 1995 appearance on *The Tonight Show with Jay Leno*.

Shock DJ Howard Stern had become very popular in the increasing contentious 1990s. His sidekick, Robin Quivers, was Leno's other guest on the night Linda Ronstadt was booked. Following her performance of 'The Waiting', she sat down between Leno and Quivers and instigated a hostile debate over Stern's morality. Linda snidely announced to Quivers, "You're schilling for him and I think he's taking advantage of you!" She was booed heavily from the audience and the evening's programming was

★ ★ ★

cut short. The spectacle provoked a considerable reaction in the press.

It was during this time that Linda made a surprising move, returning to her childhood home of Tucson, Arizona. She had arrived at the notion that Old Pueblo could be a more civilized locale for her kids to be raised. She also owned property up in the mountains of Sweetwater, Arizona. She gave an in depth interview to *Mojo* magazine, announcing her return to her hometown. She still maintained her posh San Francisco residence for another couple of years though. (In another surprise move, the intensely private Ronstadt would allow her home to be featured and photographed in extensive color detail in *Architectural Digest* magazine in 2004.)

Just three months after the release of *Feels Like Home,* a very sad and painful day came to pass for the Ronstadts. Family patriarch Gilbert Ronstadt passed away on the seventeenth of June, a mere three days after his eighty-fourth birthday. Despite this latest incident of grief, Linda was committed to a series of concert dates throughout America to promote her new album. Having always prided herself on being a staunchly proficient business woman, in stoic fashion she fulfilled her professional obligations that year.

SINGING LULLABIES

Although she was rolling along with her career, still actively recording – averaging her standard album per year – and touring, Linda was relishing the joy of being a single mother. As of 1996, she was feeling more complacent regarding the musical landscape she had covered. She was struck with another 'new' audio concept: recording a collection of classic Rock & Roll songs reinterpreted as lullabies. The notion had actually occurred to her in the early part of the decade but she had too many irons on the fire then to get down to it.

When the time did arrive to start working on the new project, Linda had a recording studio set up in her home. She was thus able to record in a relaxed atmosphere without having to leave her kids. Mary and Carlos would, of course, wander into the studio periodically to check out what their mom was up to. Ever the artistically innovative one, she even incorporated the sounds of her daughter's pacifier and her son's heartbeat – on her remake of Queen's chanting 'We Will Rock You' – into the mixes. She even featured baby Carlos on her new album cover.

Upon discovering the joy of motherhood, Ronstadt expanded her family when she adopted a baby boy in early 1994. She named her son Carlos Sangria.

She recorded classic tracks made famous from the Beach Boys, the Ronettes, and the Beatles, among others, to include on her new disc *Dedicated To The One I Love*. To promote the project she made the rounds of the current talk shows – including a return appearance on *Regis & Kathie Lee* – to increase its potential audience. (Due to the previous year's debacle, she did not return to the *Tonight Show with Jay Leno*.) The reception to the album was surprisingly strong. It reached a respectable #78 on the *Billboard* album chart, selling several hundred thousand compact discs and cassettes and gaining considerable attention. A new *Billboard* inventory, classified as the Kids Audio chart, listed the album at #1.

Shortly before *Dedicated* hit the market, Linda was contacted by representatives of the White House. President Bill Clinton and his wife, Hillary, requested that she perform a live concert for them in the White

House Rose Garden in early May. Even with her growing reputation as something of a temperamental diva run amok, she was still a legendary star with an enormous fan base.

She agreed to do a live, televised concert – and even invited Aaron Neville to come and sing with her – for the prestigious event. During the event she exclaimed to her elite audience, "I have two bands and I get to sing with Aaron Neville. I'm the luckiest girl in the world!" The buoyant show was later broadcast as a highly rated program on PBS.

One of the most illustrious career highlights for Linda Ronstadt was being asked to sing for President Bill Clinton and First Lady Hillary Clinton at The White House in 1996. She invited Aaron Neville to join her on several of their classic duets. It was broadcast on the PBS channel.

Dedicated To The One I Love became known among Linda Ronstadt fans as *The Lullaby Album*. It went on to win her yet another Grammy – her ninth – in yet another category: Best Musical Album For Children. Even in the new millennium when record companies were deleting physical availability of catalog items that were not monster sellers, *Dedicated* remained in print and in 2008 was reissued on Rhino's Flashback label

★ ★ ★

shortly before the label vanished.

Linda scheduled a major tour for the summer of 1996 and hit the road to play a series of high profile venues throughout America. Among her bookings were an August 5 concert at the historic Meadow Brook Music Festival in Rochester, Michigan and a show at Cleveland, Ohio's massive Gund Arena. The Meadow Brook date was sold out when an unexpected cancellation was announced. It was revealed that Ronstadt was suffering from an auto-immune disorder known as Hashimoto's Disease. Due to excessive fatigue brought on by the ailment, she was unable to fulfill many of her engagements.

Linda spent most of her time at her new Tucson area home during 1997, taking care of her children and regaining energy lost to her health condition. There was no new album release that year. She would have delighted in retiring as this point, but had a recording contract to fulfill as well as additional creative endeavors.

She felt relaxed and at home living back in her old home town. In September, Real Estate Agent Elizabeth Pfau of Hill & Company Realtors – the premier brokerage firm of the Bay Area – placed Linda's lavender San Francisco turn of the century Victorian specimen on the market, with a sale price of $5.8 million. The mansion was sold in a timely manner. Her manager, Ira Koslow, told reporter Diana Walsh of the *San Francisco Examiner* at the time, "She loves it in San Francisco. It's just sometimes you feel like you want to raise your kids where you were raised. It just seems silly to keep two houses."

The next year saw the release of Ronstadt's *We Ran*, a return to the Classic Rock sound synonymous with much of her 1970s and early 1980s output. Since Peter Asher's departure from her production work several years back, she'd been handling most her own producing duties herself. In 1998, she teamed with established British producer Glyn Johns who hired Tom Petty's band, The Heartbreakers, to accompany the singing legend on her latest record.

With record sales at an all-time apex during the second half of the 1990s, *We Ran* was issued just in time for the summer of 1998. However, Linda was not well enough to take on another road trip so there was no tour and no personal appearances to support the album. Without promotion, *We Ran* failed commercially – her poorest selling new studio album in a quarter century – despite being a solid album with the singer in rocking fine form. The superstar was also suffering from sleep apnea and had been admitted to the Tuscon Medical Center for additional tests that year. It was all a real shame and a disappointment to her public as they worried for her health.

TRIO REUNION – AT LAST

Following the drama that surrounded the proposed 1994 reunion of the Linda/Dolly/Emmy Lou triumvirate, Parton's parts were scrapped and all three superstars got back to their respective careers. Among the truly spectacular tracks that had been recorded for the project was Neil Young's mystical 'After The Gold Rush'. Replacing Dolly's sumptuous vocal was long time session and background singer Valerie Carter. Available on Linda's heralded 1995 return to Country Rock – a musical style that she had pioneered a quarter century earlier – the performance on *Feels Like Home* paled in comparison.

Also included on the above mentioned album were the shimmering 'High Sierra' as well as Randy Newman's solemn 'Feels Like Home' from his acclaimed musical score Faust, the old timey Carter family composition 'Lover's Return', and the deeply reflective 'The Blue Train' which was picked up by Adult Contemporary radio as an album cut and spent ten weeks on the chart's Top 40.

Luckily for everyone, during the next few years, Harris, Ronstadt, and Parton were able to reconcile their personal differences and resume their decades-old friendship. It also turned out to be a wise career move as all three were experiencing sagging record sales during the second half of the 1990s.

In the first month of the final year of the twentieth century, *Trio Two* was finally released to the public and became an instant hit. Driven by an extensive promotional tour in which the threesome were all over television talk shows, and an appealing music video for 'After The Gold

★ ★ ★

Rush' that the ladies filmed in a historic New York synagogue, the *Trio Two* album debuted in the Top Five of *Billboard*'s Country albums chart, crossed over to a worthy #62 on the main *Billboard* album chart, and returned all three veterans to the Gold standard.

The Grammy Award-winning 1987 Trio *album was a landmark event. Folling a number of setbacks, Linda, Dolly, and Emmy Lou were finally reunited for* Trio Two. *Their ethereal version of 'After The Gold Rush' won the Grammy for Best Country Vocal Collaboration in 2000. The ladies are shown here in 1999.*

It was a welcomed return indeed as music critics and the public alike praised the poignant songs on the popular release. On 'After The Gold Rush', Valerie Carter's voice was replaced with Dolly's opulent lead and the music video was shown in heavy rotation on Country music-related cable channels. To no one's surprise, *Trio Two* was nominated for several Grammy Awards the following year including the Best Country Album. When 'Gold Rush' was awarded the trophy for Best Country Vocal Collaboration, it brought Linda Ronstadt's number of Grammy wins to an astounding ten. (In 2000, that number was surpassed by only Aretha Franklin, Ella Fitzgerald, and Leontyne Price.)

Now that the women had rejuvenated their careers, Ronstadt and

Harris commenced with a project they had long contemplated. They decided to record a charming 'duo' album comprised of Folkish-styled tunes. Still dealing with her affliction of Hashimoto's Disease, Linda was reluctant to leave the Tucson area and her young children. As the twentieth century came to an end, she told Jan Ramsey in *Off Beat* magazine,

> "I have children and I'm a stay at home mom. That's what
> I want to do with my life and I'm very happy doing it."

Instead of leaving town, she and Emmy took up residence in a luxury suite in Tucson's Arizona Inn.

The album that resulted from their local vacation was titled *Western Wall-The Tucson Sessions*. Issued a mere seven months after the smash *Trio Two*, it was nearly as successful. It was even nominated for a Grammy in the Best Contemporary Folk Album category. *Western Wall* eventually achieved sales of close to 400,000 copies.

Following the album's release, Ronstadt and Harris embarked on a tour of exclusive venues. It was Linda's first time on the road in several years and, in typical fashion, she made a point of voicing her reluctance to touring in the press. She lamented to Jan Ramsey,

> "I gave up touring...I was so happy to let it go. If it wer-
> en't for Emmy Lou Harris, I wouldn't do this. If I weren't
> such a deep fan of Emmy's and love her company and
> really have great confidence in her ability to always make
> musical sense, I would never even have considered this."

The bookings, ironically, were only on the West and East Coasts. To the disappointment of their fans, there were no dates scheduled for the north or the mid-west.

From the mid-1990s forward, Linda moved toward downsizing the size of the concert halls that she performed in. She still maintained a substantial live audience. It was a real treat for her fans to be able to see and hear her in more intimate settings. There was a down side, however. Since there were fewer seats at her current gigs, she charged astronomi-

★ ★ ★

cally high ticket prices. Having to meet her reported $80,000 to $90,000 required fee per performance, there was considerable dissention among her fan base because of it.

Although she was pleased to finally have the opportunity to go out with her old friend and musical sister, Linda claimed that she would never tour again after the *Western Wall* shows were over. Emmy Lou told journalist Mark Watson, following a 2000 concert in Pontiac, Michigan, "Linda is wonderful, but I don't think we'll see her out on the road ever again. She hates it!"

Linda Ronstadt was now looking forward to an 'official' retirement. She had no interest in re-signing with her record label after the expiration of her contract in 2000. She could look back over her long career and claim the accomplishment of far more than most artists could ever dream of. Back in the 1970s, at her initial career peak, it had never even occurred to her that she would experience such longevity in such a fickle business.

★ ★ ★

★ ★ ★

9

Retirement and Political Activism

As Linda Ronstadt entered the new millennium, she could claim the position of being one of the most successful female entertainers of the Twentieth Century. In the year 2000, she had enjoyed twenty-three years with the same record company. She now owed them just one final album to finish out her contract.

Although she had seemingly covered every possible musical style, the one thing Linda had never tackled was a Christmas album. Despite having loved a number of traditional holiday songs over the years, she had simply never gotten around to recording any of them. John Boylan reentered the scene to produce her first release of the new millennium. For her final release with Elektra Entertainment, Linda released *A Merry Little Christmas.*

Having employed the choir of the University Of Arizona, she set about recording a shimmering mixture of compositions commemorating the Christmas season. Linda's holiday record was important for another reason. Back in the Eighties, while working with Nelson Riddle, she became friendly with Rosemary Clooney. Rosemary, the aunt of Academy Award winning actor George Clooney, was one of the most popular singers of the 1950s. In 2000, the two pals from different generations recorded a duet version of the classic 'White Christmas'. It was an especially poignant event since Rosemary died of lung cancer in June of 2002.

★ ★ ★

A Merry Little Christmas peaked at a very modest #179 on *Billboard's* album chart. Although it was not a huge seller, it remains an in-print catalog item and continues to move a respectable number of copies each holiday season.

When the Twenty-First Century arrived, Linda Ronstadt had more than accomplished her projected goals. Despite having a comfortable life, there had been some severe bumps in the road along with her journey. In the late 1990s, Linda became the object of a deranged stalker's affections. Robert Ortiz had become obsessed with the singer to the point of having a serious break with reality.

For several years the singer was unnerved by his brazen attempts at contacting her as well as other Ronstadt relatives. He had mailed bizarre gifts and letters to her. The menace reportedly even showed up at Mike Ronstadt's Tucson area home in a futile attempt at gaining access to Linda. She went through legal channels to ascertain a restraining order against him. Unfortunately, Ortiz violated the order numerous times and was subsequently incarcerated. Fearing for the safety of her young children and other family members, it did little to quell her discomfort.

She had, however, become complacent with her status as a retiree and stay-at-home parent. Delighting in her return to a quiet existence in Tucson, she found herself contented with her life. Consequentially, she was largely absent from the limelight for the next few years.

She did make some appearances on friend's recordings during this semi-hiatus. For instance, she was prominently featured on *Evangeline Made,* an album of Cajun music, with Ann Savoy. They would later team up for a duo album. She also sang a duet with her good chum Bette Midler in 2003. They collaborated on the track 'Sisters' on the Gold-certified *Bette Midler Sings The Rosemary Clooney Song Book.*

Linda also found time to produce a disc of Classical music performed by Dennis James, the glass armonica player she had discovered in 1993. His work was featured prominently on her *Winter Light* album that year. The 2002 release was entitled *Cristal: Glass Music Through The Ages.* James had made numerous appearances with her on the *Winter Light* tour and played on subsequent recordings of hers as well.

★ ★ ★

Linda first discovered the unique glass armonica instrument in the late 1970s. A decade and a half later, she located virtuoso glass armonica player Dennis James. She hired him to play on numerous recordings beginning with her archetypal Winter Light *album. In 2002, she produced the iridescent Dennis James album* Cristal – Glass Music Through The Ages.

In the interim, Rhino Records, the foremost reissue label in the business and an affiliate of the Warner Brothers umbrella, issued their first Linda Ronstadt product. Entitled *The Very Best Of Linda Ronstadt*, it encompassed her hit singles and best known album cuts from 'Different Drum' in 1967 through 'Winter Light' in 1993. It was a Top 20 Country album that lasted well over a year on the chart and climbed the Pop albums chart as well. It also stands as an excellent single disc testimony to her long hit making streak. In fact, when *Rolling Stone* published their *500 Greatest Albums of All Time*, the disc ranked at #320.

After being at home for several years, she once again got the itch to make music. Nearly twenty years after the death of Nelson Riddle, Linda decided to return to her beloved Jazz standards once more.

Enlisting the cream of the crop of the Contemporary Jazz cognoscenti, she embarked on her official return to the genre in 2003. The major variable being that this time she was under no stress of deadlines from a record company. Having concluded her relationship with Elektra in 2000, she was now a free agent.

In early 2004, well before completion of her album, Linda Ronstadt signed a brand new recording contract with the historic Jazz label, Verve Records. That spring and summer, she embarked on her first major tour since 1999 in anticipation of the forthcoming recording.

RONSTADT RETURNS TO JAZZ

Hummin' To Myself, Ronstadt's first new studio album since *A Merry Little Christmas* and her first Jazz product since *For Sentimental Reasons,* finally saw the light of day in November of 2004. Although it attracted little attention from contemporary record buyers and radio stations, it debuted on *Billboard*'s Contemporary Jazz chart at an invigorating #2 in its first week on the market.

Production duties for *Hummin' To Myself* were handled by John Boylan and George Massenburg. The recording sessions took place in Hollywood, Nashville, and at The Club House on Upper Hook Road in Rhinebeck, New York – about 100 miles north of the city. The artist and musicians who participated in the recording could not have been more pleased with the results. It spent half a year on the Jazz listing and sold 75,000 US copies within its first year – which was actually respectable for a small independent label release from a veteran artist.

Although it was originally announced that Ronstadt's Verve contract was for "several albums over the next several years", *Hummin' To Myself* was her sole release with the company. No information was publicly disclosed regarding the reason why her tenure with Verve was cut short.

Less than two years later, she was on the Vanguard recording label for her duet album with Ann Savoy. That also turned out to be a one shot. Sadly, her Cajun exploration, *Adieu False Heart,* would mark the final new Linda Ronstadt release as her health would take a staid downturn in the ensuing years.

In stark contradiction to her well known aversion to touring, Linda spent the better part of 2006 traveling and doing live concerts for enthusiastic fans. It seemed unlikely that she needed the money but, with an

★ ★ ★

economy in free fall, anything was possible. Either way, the singer wasn't giving any explanations to anyone. In the year she turned sixty, she was back on the road doing what she does best. Having long since tired of gargantuan arenas and pavilions, she booked exclusive dates in a series of small, intimate venues.

In 2004, Linda Ronstadt and Aaron Neville headlined a show at Detroit's legendary Music Hall Center For The Performing Arts in honor or the celebrated site's seventy-fifth anniversary. The building is located across the street from the Detroit Athletic League where Linda's grandfather, Lloyd Copeman, was a charter member.

One of Ronstadt's final live appearances was in San Diego at Humphrey's By The Bay in July of 2006. Regrettably, she was forced to cancel many of her subsequent bookings due to female health issues. She was admitted to a Tucson hospital that summer for surgery and consequently made good on her promise to avoid live performing with a few isolated exceptions.

Shortly before celebrating her sixtieth birthday, Linda purchased another swanky – although less elaborate – dwelling in San Francisco. According to Joel Selvin of the *San Francisco Chronicle*, in 2006, she was

★ ★ ★

"trying to adjust to the smaller quarters of an upstairs duplex." After selling her Victorian mansion in 1997 for nearly $6 million, the superstar bought another domicile at 3485 Washington Street in the adjoining Laurel Heights district of the city, near the area known as Little Italy. Selvin stated at the time, "She lived across the street from her current residence...Her kids walk to school and she feels comfortable strolling the shops in her neighborhood."

Linda and Aaron with John Boylan backstage at Detroit's intimate Music Hall. It was the night of the historic venue's annual Cars & Stars event. It also marked Ronstadt's final concert performance in Michigan.

However, even shortly after her move back, Ronstadt was restless and "looking for properties around Laurel Heights that might be roomier... but real estate prices in that neighborhood gone through the stratosphere." According to web site Zillow.com, the 2,289 square foot lot residence, built in 1911, has three bedrooms and two baths, and was listed for $1,950,000 on April 11, 2010 and sold for the asking price in thirteen days.

Subsequently, Linda moved to another area home that, according to Public Record, sold for $1,990,000 on July 23, 2009. This adobe has "four bedrooms, three baths, near the Sea Cliff gates, with a walk out garden,

★ ★ ★

master suite with deck, legal/non-conforming self-contained studio cottage…two fireplaces, laundry room, radiant heat, hardwood floors."

Yet not long afterward, Ronstadt told the *Arizona Daily Star,*

> "I leased my house out in Tucson. But I stop off in Tucson on my way to Mexico. It's a good pit stop on the way to Mexico. I love going to Mexico. I've been spending time in northern Mexico and I really love it."

LEGACY OF THE ROCK QUEEN

She is no longer regarded as a current or contemporary public figure but the influence of Linda Ronstadt resonates though the annals of time. She was largely responsible for pioneering the hybrid of the Country Rock musical genre. She was the first female recording star of any genre to sell out mammoth stadiums and arenas throughout the world. She continually shattered records as the first woman to consistently sell Platinum or better with every album release. In summation, Linda was the first woman in the Rock genus to achieve equal status in what was – in the Seventies – an exclusively male domain.

There are a number of Linda Ronstadt tribute bands in existence today, including Blue Bayou with singer Robyn Roth, a Los Angeles band known as the West Coasters, and Simple Dreams with attractive brunette singer Jill Morrison. They exclusively play covers of Ronstadt tunes. Female singers from multiple fields of entertainment continue to acknowledge Linda's influence on them in developing their own sonic signatures.

In 2007, Linda was inducted into the Arizona Music & Entertainment Hall of Fame. To the disappointment of the event planners, she was a no show at the event, instead sending one of her nephews to accept the honor on her behalf.

In 2008, Ronstadt was the recipient of a special Trailblazer's Award from the American Latino Media Arts (ALMA). Numerous recording stars serenaded her that evening, performing Linda's classic hits as she watched from the front row.

The following year, she was honored in a huge, celebrity filled, televised presentation with a special ALMA (American Latino Media Arts) 'Trailblazers Award'. As stated by Tony Partridge on his Linda Ronstadt Home Page web site, "ALMA was formed in 1995 to honor Hispanic performers and promote positive images of Hispanics in entertainment." On August 17, 2008, Linda Ronstadt was saluted by eminent Opera tenor Placido Domingo. During the presentation, several popular singers – including Wynonna Judd and Detroit's BeBe Winans – performed her hits in tribute to her. This homage was especially personal to Linda as it acknowledged not only her talent but her heritage as well.

The tributes continue to roll out in her honor. In the spring of 2009, Ronstadt was awarded an honorary doctorate degree from the Berklee College of Music in Boston, Massachusetts. Reporting on the accolade, *Mix* magazine summated, "Linda Ronstadt (has) left her mark on more than the record business. Her devotion to the craft of singing (has) influ-

★ ★ ★

enced many audio professionals." The article went on to state that Linda is "intensely knowledgeable about the mechanics of singing and the cultural contexts of every genre she passes."

In 2009, Linda Ronstadt was honored with an honorary Doctorate's Degree from the esteemed Berklee College of Music in Boston, Massachusetts.

That same year, the Martin Guitar Company, located in Nazareth, Pennsylvania, manufactured and issued their 'Linda Ronstadt Limited Edition 00-42' acoustic model. Linda donated all proceeds from sales of the instrument to the Land Institute, based in Salina, Kansas.

In early 2010, Ronstadt joined thousands of protesters in her hometown. The crowd was assembled for Tucson's National Day of Action. They were demonstrating against alleged mistreatment of illegal aliens, fighting Arizona's anti-immigrant laws.

Just three months later, in April of 2010, she campaigned against Arizona's new anti-immigration law, SB 1070. Linda spoke out, declaring, "This is a devastating blow to law enforcement. The police don't protect us in a democracy with brute force."

In 2011, she was awarded the Lifetime Achievement Grammy from the Latin Recording Academy. Having won eleven competitive NARAS statues – in addition to several American Music Awards and Country Music Association Awards – her stature and influence on the music community were again recognized by her peers.

Over the course of her nearly half-century as a recording artist, Linda has won an amazing total of 11 competitive Grammy Awards in various categories. In 2011, she was honored again. This time it was with a Lifetime Achievement Grammy. She is shown here with Neil Portnow, the current President of the Recording Academy.

Linda is also an outspoken advocate of the arts and for the environment. She has even stoutly criticized the current leaders of Tucson, declaring, "The local city council's failings, developer's strip mall mentality, greed, and a growing dust problem have rendered the city unrecognizable and poorly developed."

LINDA RONSTADT NOW

Upon announcing her retirement, following her last public concert performance in 2009, Linda Ronstadt was enjoying her retirement and her life. She became a connoisseur of ballet and loved going out to the theatre for her personal enjoyment. After many decades of performing for others, she was taking   pleasure in letting others entertain her.

Her brother, Mike, quantified in 2011, "She's done. She's through.

★ ★ ★

She's completely retired. She's not doing any more tours. She's not doing any more live shows." As far back as 2006, Joel Selvin reported that, "Ronstadt is…without management, a real record deal or even her own web site. She has no publicity representatives or handlers outside of her crisply efficient personal assistant."

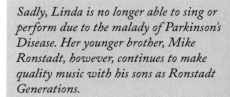

Sadly, Linda is no longer able to sing or perform due to the malady of Parkinson's Disease. Her younger brother, Mike Ronstadt, however, continues to make quality music with his sons as Ronstadt Generations.

Her kids are happy, healthy, and now entering young adulthood. Her daughter, Mary, now 23, graduated from high school in the year 2009 and still resides with her legendary mom. Linda's son, Carlos, is a bespectacled twenty year old who, ironically, resembles a cross between Buddy Holly and Elvis Costello. He graduated high school in 2012 and now lives in Santa Cruz, California – approximately 80 miles south of San Fran – with his longtime girlfriend. Carlos himself is also musical with a wide range of artistic interests and abilities. When he turned eighteen in January of 2012, he set about locating his birth parents. Succeeding in short order, he has now established a strong relationship with them and subsequently changed his name to Carlos Graves.

As Mike Ronstadt told Music Historian Mark Watson in 2012, "Mary and Carlos have both graduated from high school and are getting ready

★ ★ ★

to make their own way in the world. Carlos is currently taking a year off to work while he decides what he wants to do with his life."

Certainly Linda realizes how fortunate she is to have reveled in the recompenses of such a privileged life – and to still be here. Many of her closest friends and musical compatriots have passed away at young ages.

Her long time keyboard player, Don Grolnick, died of lymphoma in 1996 at just 47, her *protégée* and former Brentwood roommate, Nicolette Larson, died of cerebral edema in 1997 at only 45. Her old drummer, Mike Botts, passed on from colon cancer in 2005. He was 61 years old. Kenny Edwards lost his life to cancer as well, in 2010, at 64. A long time singing friend and supporter, Phoebe Snow, passed away from complications following a stroke in the spring of 2011 when she was 60. The most recent major loss was her beloved "Android" – Andrew Gold. He died of heart failure in his sleep in June of 2011 at age 59.

In July of 2011, the month that she turned 65, it was announced that Linda Ronstadt had signed a contract – for an undisclosed sum but purported to be in the millions – with legendary publishing house Simon & Schuster to pen her autobiography. It was revealed,

> "Simon & Schuster has announced it will publish Linda Ronstadt's memoir, *Heart Like A Wheel*. The (autobiography) is named after the eleven-time Grammy Award-winning singer's fifth album…The publication date is tentatively scheduled for 2013…Simon & Schuster says the book will trace Ronstadt's rise in the music industry and her career as a trail-blazing woman in contemporary music. Linda Ronstadt has sold over 100 million records worldwide."

As the book was being readied for release, an announcement was made that shocked the world. In August of 2013, it was revealed that Linda Ronstadt had been diagnosed – the previous December – with the incapacitating Parkinson's Disease, a movement disorder characterized by tremor(s), muscle rigidity, and slow and imprecise movement. The disclosure promoted an outpouring of public attention and career acknowledgements that followed.

★ ★ ★

The appellation of her autobiography had been changed to *Simple Dreams – A Musical Memoir.* It hit the bookstores and websites in September of 2013. Although decidedly prim and conservative in content, it was handsomely extolled and went over big with the public. It debuted in the Top 10 of *The New York Times* Best Sellers list – an uncommon accomplishment for a musician's story.

Simultaneously, Ronstadt found herself back in the headlines in a tidal wave of publicity. She was featured on the cover of *People* magazine for the first time since the 1980s. Esteemed television anchorwoman Diane Sawyer interviewed her for an episode of 20/20. *Goldmine* magazine spotlighted her – yet again – and she was featured in two separate *Goldmine* cover stories (November 2013 and June 2014). She also appeared again on *Tavis Smiley* in a two-part feature. Throughout her latest challenge she has remained stoic and valiant.

On April 10, 2014 Linda Ronstadt received the most stellar honor of her career when she was inducted into The Rock & Roll Hall Of Fame. Her official inductor was her former band mate, Glenn Frey, who – along with longtime friends Stevie Nicks, Bonnie Raitt and EmmyLou Harris – performed a moving musical tribute to Linda. Also inducted during the evening's ceremonial at Brooklyn's Barclays Center were Nirvana, Daryl Hall & John Oates, Kiss, Peter Gabriel, Bruce Springsteen's E Street Band, and – with some trepidation – Cat Stevens.

Immediately afterward, Linda returned to the *Billboard* album chart with the newly released *Duets,* a compilation – including one unreleased track from the vaults – that featured various collaborative efforts spanning several decades. It hit #32, marking her highest album position since *Cry Like A Rainstorm-Howl Like The Wind* nearly a quarter century ago.

Yet another honor was bequeathed upon Linda Ronstadt in 2014 when the Library Of Congress entered her *Heart Like A Wheel* album into the NRR (National Recording Registry) as a historical work of art. Linda was only the third female recording artist ever to receive such an astonishing commendation (following Judy Garland and Carole King).

On July 28, 2014, Linda bravely traveled to our nation's capital, Washington D. C., in her wheel chair. She was wheeled into the Oval Office inside the White House where President Barack Obama awarded her the National Medal of Arts. President Obama was the third American president to single out Miss Ronstadt for a special event. The honors continue to roll out in recognition of the singer's resonance and hard work as well as her lasting influence as a pioneering and brilliant person and artist.

As conspicuously disclosed on CelebrityNetWorth.com, Ronstadt is one of the wealthiest women in the entertainment business with assets of - an astronomical - $115 million dollars.

In the mid-1990s, Linda returned to Tucson with her two little children and purchased this stately Mediterranean-styled home. Although she moved back to San Francisco in 2006, she maintained her Tucson domicile until 2014 when she placed it back on the market.

Linda Ronstadt started her career as a shy and insecure but driven eighteen year old college dropout, coming to a gargantuan city in search of fame. She persevered, obtaining a major recording contract, and persisted in relentlessly advancing her talents. After years of being the industry's most successful female artist, she was not contented with the confines of her fertile musical style. She incessantly branched out, challenging her abilities and broadening her phenomenal talents. In the process, she experienced major success in nearly every imaginable musical genre.

★ ★ ★

As her one-time employee, Don Henley, stated to CMT (Country Music Television) in 2000, "Linda was a pioneer." She forged the way for women in the music business to become more in control of their own destiny and careers. She accomplished this by always being true to her own beliefs and ambitions, exploring the styles that motivated her. Strong-willed, passionate, and powerful, Ronstadt became a consummate role model for those who followed. Never once did the pressures and distractions of fame and celebrity get on top of her. For decades she conducted a high-powered career on her own terms.

As Linda told writer Randal Hill for the publication *Superstars Of Rock* at the height of her eminence,

> "I'm a survivor...That doesn't mean you have to be made of steel. It means you must be on your own side. You have to want to win."

★ ★ ★

SELECTED DISCOGRAPHY

1967	*The Stone Poneys*
1967	*Evergreen, Volume Two*
1968	*Stone Poneys And Friends, Volume Three*
1969	*Hand Sown…Home Grown*
1970	*Silk Purse*
1972	*Linda Ronstadt*
1973	*Don't Cry Now*
1974	*Heart Like A Wheel*
1975	*Prisoner In Disguise*
1976	*Hasten Down The Wind*
1977	*Simple Dreams*
1978	*Living In The USA*
1980	*Mad Love*
1981	*The Pirates Of Penzance (Original Soundtrack)*
1982	*Get Closer*
1983	*What's New*
1984	*Lush Life*
1986	*For Sentimental Reasons*
1987	*Trio*
1987	*Canciones De Mi Padre*
1989	*Cry Like A Rainstorm, Howl Like The Wind*
1991	*Mas Canciones*
1992	*Frenesi*
1993	*Winter Light*
1995	*Feels Like Home*
1996	*Dedicated To The One I Love*
1998	*We Ran*
1999	*Trio Two*
1999	*Western Wall – The Tucson Sessions*
2000	*A Merry Little Christmas*
2004	*Hummin' To Myself*
2006	*Adieu False Heart*

★ ★ ★

CHRONOLOGY

1946 Maria Linda Ronstadt is born in Tucson, Arizona

1960 Linda enters the new Catalina High School after attending a Catholic Parochial School from first through eighth grades

1960 Linda performs around Tucson with her sister, Suzi, and older brother, Peter, as The New Union Ramblers. They meet local musician, Bobby Kimmel

1964 At year's end, Linda leaves Tucson for Los Angeles, California after having visited LA several times during the year

1966 Linda forms The Stone Poneys band with Kimmel and LA musician Kenny Edwards. The group signs with Capitol Records and records their first album

1967 The Stone Poneys record and release their second album, which includes their first major hit, 'Different Drum'

1969 Succeeding the disbandment of The Poneys, Ronstadt begrudgingly becomes a solo artist. Her first solo album tanks

1970 Linda records a deliberate attempt at Country music in Nashville, Tennessee. The album includes her first major solo hit, 'Long Long Time'. The emotional ballad is nominated for a Grammy Award in a superstar lineup

1975 After many years of ups and downs, Linda Ronstadt becomes a superstar with her five-star album, *Heart Like A Wheel*. It becomes the first in a record-breaking streak of hugely successful recordings that establish Ronstadt as the biggest female singer in the music industry

1977 Linda scores one of the biggest selling albums in record history to date with *Simple Dreams*, which tops the Pop and Country albums charts. She is featured on the covers of *Time*, *People*, and *Rolling Stone*

★ ★ ★

1978	Linda makes her motion picture debut in *FM*. She releases her chart-topping *Living In The USA* disc which has an advance order of 2.1 million copies – the highest of any album in history to date
1980	Tired of the grind of playing huge stadiums and arenas, the First Lady of Rock moves to New York City to star in Gilbert & Sullivan's century old Operetta, *The Pirates Of Penzance*. Her boyfriend, Governor Jerry Brown, runs for President of the United States
1983	After returning to Rock & Roll for one last album and major Rock tour, Linda transitions into Big Band Jazz. *What's New* establishes a new image and audience for her. It also pioneers a new trend in the recording industry
1984	Linda takes on a full-fledged Opera, starring as Mimi in Puccini's classic *La Boheme* while continuing her success as a Jazz diva
1987	Following the unexpected death of her mentor, Nelson Riddle, Linda continues to expand her singing abilities with movie soundtracks, traditional Country, and the music of her childhood and family roots, Mexican Mariachi
1989	After her move to San Francisco, California, Ronstadt gets together with Aaron Neville of the New Orleans R&B group, The Neville Brothers. The duo become a huge Multi-Platinum, Grammy Award winning success
1990	Linda Ronstadt adopts a baby girl at year's end. She names the child Mary Clementine. Linda subsequently looks for a way to slow down her hectic career
1993	After returning to the Spanish language for more albums, Linda records a New Age-styled record, *Winter Light*. It is regarded as one of greatest career albums
1994	Exultant with her single parent status, Ronstadt adopts a baby boy. She names him Carlos Sangria

★ ★ ★

1996   Linda records a Grammy Award-winning album of classic Rock & Roll songs, reinterpreted as children lullabies. She relocates back to Tucson with her little children

1999   Linda Ronstadt reunites with Country superstars Dolly Parton and Emmy Lou Harris for another smash *Trio project*. Ronstadt and Harris record and release a duo album and hit the road for a series of live concert appearances

2000   Linda records an ethereal Christmas album which finishes her contract with Elektra/Asylum

2004   Ronstadt signs a new recording contract with Verve Records and returns to the Jazz music genre with *Hummin' To Myself*. She also returns to major touring during this era

2006   Linda mysteriously turns up on Vanguard Records with *Adieu False Heart*, recorded with Cajun singer, Ann Savoy. It turns out to be her final new album release

2011   The National Academy of Recording Arts & Sciences (NARAS) honors Linda Ronstadt with her eleventh Grammy Award – this time for Lifetime Achievement

2013   Linda shocks the world when she reveals her diagnosis of the debilitating Parkinson's Disease. She releases her autobiography, *Simple Dreams – A Musical Memoir*, which debuts in the Top 10 of *The New York Times* Best Sellers List. The public rallies in support of the legendary superstar.

2014   Linda Ronstadt is inducted into The Rock & Roll Hall Of Fame. She releases her highest charting album in 24 years with *Duets*. The Library of Congress enters Linda's magnum opus *Heart Like A Wheel* into the National Recording Registry. President Barack Obama personally awards Miss Ronstadt the National Medal of Arts.

★ ★ ★

LINDA RONSTADT GRAMMY AWARDS

1975   Best Country Vocal Performance – Female / 'I Can't Help It (If I'm Still In Love With You)'

1976   Best Pop Vocal Performance – Female / *Hasten Down The Wind* (album)

1980   Best Recording For Children / *In Harmony - A Sesame Street Record* (album)

1987   Best Country Performance – Duo or Group with Vocal / *Trio* (album) – with Dolly Parton and EmmyLou Harris

1988   Best Mexican-American Performance / *Canciones De Mi Padre* (album)

1989   Best Pop Performance – Duo or Group with Vocal / 'Don't Know Much' – with Aaron Neville

1990   Best Pop Performance – Duo or Group with Vocal / 'All My Life' – with Aaron Neville

1992   Best Mexican-American Album / *Mas Canciones* (album)

1992   Best Tropical Latin Album / *Frenesi* (album)

1996   Best Musical Album For Children / *Dedicated To The One I Love* (album)

1999   Best Country Vocal Collaboration / 'After The Gold Rush' – with EmmyLou Harris and Dolly Parton

2011   Lifetime Achievement

★ ★ ★

FURTHER RESOURCES

BOOKS

Romanowski, Patricia, and Holly George-Warren, and Jon Parales. *The Rolling Stone Encyclopedia of Rock & Roll*. San Francisco, California: Fireside, 2005.

Amdur, Melissa. *Hispanics of Achievement / Linda Ronstadt / Singer*. Philadelphia, Pennsylvania: Chelsea House, 2001.

Kingsbury, Paul, and Michael McCall, and John Rumble. *The Encyclopedia of Country Music*. New York: Oxford, 2012.

Bufwack, Mary, and Robert Oermann. *Finding Her Voice / Women in Country Music, 1800-2000*. Nashville, Tennesee: The Country Music Foundation and Vanderbilt University, 2003.

Rosen, Craig. *The Billboard Book of Number One Albums*. New York: Billboard Books, 1996.

O'Dair, Barbara. *Trouble Girls / The Rolling Stone Book of Women in Rock*. New York: Random House, 1997.

★ ★ ★

WEB SITES

The Linda Ronstadt Home Page
www.ronstadt-linda.com

The Rock & Roll Hall of Fame: Linda Ronstadt
www.rockhall.com

The Country Music Hall of Fame: Linda Ronstadt
www.countrymusichalloffame.org

About the Author

Mark Watson is a musicologist as well as a freelance journalist and music historian with several decades of involvement in various capacities of entertainment. He holds numerous degrees and certifications from various institutes.

Often referred to as The Motor City Music Historian, he is currently based in the Detroit area and also spends time in California, Arizona, and Florida.

★ ★ ★

Photo Credits

The photographs featured in this publication were provided
via a number of sources, including but not limited to:

The Tony Partridge Archives and Personal Photo Collection

The Mark Watson Archives and Personal Photo Collection

The Doreen Onuski Archives and Personal Photo Collection

★ ★ ★

2014 INDUCTEE

ROCK AND ROLL
HALL OF FAME

LINDA RONSTADT

★ ★ ★

CPSIA information can be obtained at www.ICGtesting.com
Printed in the USA
LVOW02*1219200815

450886LV00001B/1/P